THE ARKANSAS

An American River

SUNSET FROM CADRON SETTLEMENT

THE

ARKANSAS

An American River

WILLIAM MILLS

THE UNIVERSITY OF ARKANSAS PRESS

FAYETTEVILLE · LONDON · 1988

DESIGNER: Chiquita Babb
TYPEFACE: Linotron 202 Caslon Old Face 2
TYPESETTER: G & S Typesetters, Inc.
PRINTER: Dai Nippon Printing Co., Ltd.
BINDER: Dai Nippon Printing Co., Ltd.

The paper used in this publication meets the minimum requirements of the
American National Standard for Permanence of Paper for Printed Library
Materials Z39.48-1984. ⊗

LIBRARY OF CONGRESS CATALOGING-IN-PUBLICATION DATA

Mills, William, 1935–
The Arkansas: an American river.

Bibliography: p.
1. River ecology—Arkansas River.   2. Natural
history—Arkansas River.   3. Arkansas River—Description
and travel.   I. Title.
QH104.5.A74M54   1988   508.767'3'0924   88-10607
ISBN 1-55728-043-6 (alk. paper)
ISBN 1-55728-044-4 (pbk.: alk. paper)

For Robert E. Lowrey
and, once again,
for Bev

ACKNOWLEDGMENTS

Right away I thank my friend Bob Lowrey for all the good times on the river. He is a skilled outdoorsman, but in addition, he can talk about art and life while prowling the rock jetties, sloughs, and bottoms. In important ways our high talk led to this book.

Joe Swyers figures significantly in the mountain section of the book, as well he should. My thanks also to Evelyn Boggs, a biologist at Colorado Mountain College in Leadville; David M. Armstrong, a leading authority on mammals at the University of Colorado at Boulder; and Bill Buckles at the University of Pueblo, for our conversation about petroglyphs. Tom and Eva Betts were my guides in Lamar, Colorado.

There are far more people in Kansas that should be acknowledged than I will be able to name specifically. My principal pathfinder there was Dave Ranney of the Harris News Service. Dave, who has roamed the state all his life and seems to know everyone there, provided me with contacts that proved invaluable. Many thanks to Fran and Troy Majors, old friends in Wichita, for help and hospitality; Mike Kelly and the Friends of the Ablah Library who invited me to talk about the river; Carl and Paul Bentrup of Deerfield; Phil Arnold of Ashland; James Lee Burke at Wichita State; Gerald Wiens and the Chaplin Nature Center; Joe Kramer and Marvin Peterson of Kansas Fish and Game; and Lisa Peterson for her hospitality.

A special thanks to Jerry Shaw, who teaches at Wichita State, but whom I associate with Gray Horse, Oklahoma, and to all the Osage of the Big Hills people. My debt to the Arkansas Natural Heritage Commission is beyond reckoning, but Bill Pell, Tom Foti, and Ken Smith are prominent in the book. Also I acknowledge Michael Hoffman and the University of Arkansas Museum; Joan Chapin, Cheryl Barr, and David Rider of the LSU Entomology Museum; and Lowell Urbatsch and Florence Givens of the LSU Herbarium in Baton Rouge for assistance with plant identifications, though any error is mine, of course. A special thanks to the flying neurosurgeon, Dr. Tom Fulbright, for help in the aerial photography, and the interesting landing at Greenville as he searched for the flaps in a strange aircraft.

For hospitality along the way, I thank Mike and Susan Nichols; Al and Gay Vekovius; and Bob Lowrey's wife Pam, who went beyond the call of duty. To my brother Thomas Finney Mills, who has carried more than his share of the loads on many river trips, I am especially grateful. I am also very happy to acknowledge the entire staff at The University of Arkansas Press; its director, Miller Williams; my editor, Martha Estes; and Chiquita Babb, who designed the book.

By now it is a ritual to thank my wife, Beverly Jarrett, for encouragement and help in all my books, and the ritual is yet alive with meaning.

CONTENTS

THE

ARKANSAS

An American River

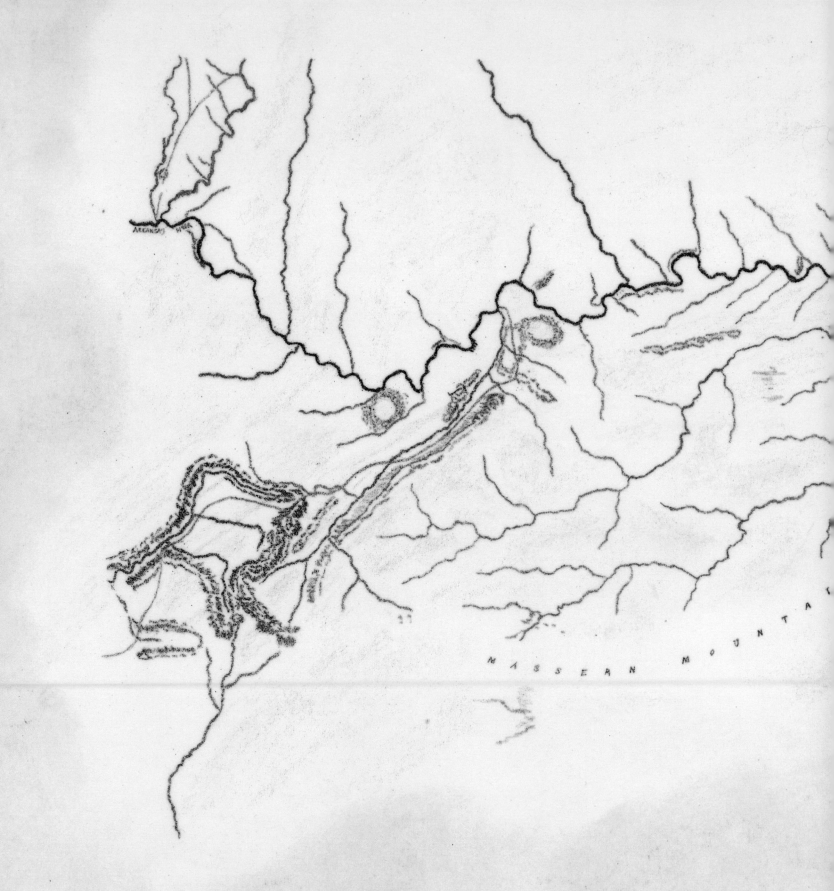

Introduction

THE ARKANSAS VALLEY WITH MT. ELBERT IN THE DISTANCE

HOW easy it is to take a river for granted. One fishes it, crosses it, drives alongside it. My early contacts with the Arkansas River were like those of most people. Of course I knew the actual river often disappeared from view and became unknown, but I had some general knowledge of it in Arkansas and Oklahoma. I mark my nascent desire to know more about this river from a day one summer when I was out fishing with a friend in his boat, somewhere above Toad Suck Dam.

In late summer the big rise of May and June is over with, the river is normally down, and sweeping sand bars make their appearance. The river moves slower then, the breeze becomes mostly a hope unless a thunderhead manages to build up, and such summer bliss works its way toward reflection and quiet talk. It was on such a day that my friend and I were fishing. He remarked that this great, wide river near Conway, Arkansas, really had its beginning in Colorado. I was taken aback and felt a little sheepish about not knowing something so basic about a river I had received so much pleasure from. Since that day I've encountered many people in Arkansas who were equally surprised. Before my travels getting to know the river were over, a man in Colorado would look up at me and exclaim, "You mean this water goes all the way to the Mississippi?"

Seeking a river's source seems fundamental to the human animal. While the palimpsest of the modern mind has largely had the tracking of game to its source or destination erased, having more urgent causalities to unroll, following a river to its genesis still has its way with us. It is not completely inexplicable that a river and its source become the metaphor for our ascent, or descent, into ourselves.

Not many months after I was first seized by the passion for the Arkansas River's source, the passion to know the entire river in a way I had not known it before, I began to realize what a large task this would be. At times I wished I might have been possessed by a shorter river. The Arkansas is roughly 1,460 miles long; its sheer length makes a single round trip, without any excursions on some of its shorter tributaries, a major undertaking. But possessed I was, and I took my first trip during the week following Christmas after that summer of fishing at Toad Suck. I decided to follow the river as well as I could by car up most of its length, picking it up around Pine Bluff, Arkansas, saving for later that portion where it finally flows across the great alluvial plain to the mouth.

This was not the prettiest time to see the river, at least not in three of the states it passes through. But it was a week I had and so I ran with the opportunity. Beyond Oklahoma I was in new territory. Soon I discovered that in many places one can't stay beside the river. From Tulsa to Wichita, you could cross it occasionally, but that was about it. At Great Bend, Kansas, where you pick up U.S. Highway 50, which runs near the river at most points, it is still not visible; one keeps track by watching for the line of cottonwoods. From Great Bend to La Junta, Colorado, the Santa Fe Trail used to run roughly along the same path, which adds a lot of romance to the history of the river. The river leaves U.S. 50 in Salida, Colorado, but beyond Cañon

City it runs alongside the highway and becomes spectacular as only a stream in the high mountains can be.

Winter offered no restraint on the beauty of Colorado. It had snowed earlier in the week but at this point the road was clear, and the white mantle only made the landscape more breathtaking. I motored through astonishing mountain canyons up to Salida. Turning north through the upper Arkansas valley I saw some of the tallest peaks in the lower forty-eight states. People of the valley proudly talk of their "fourteeners," peaks that exceed fourteen thousand feet.

Beyond Buena Vista my luck changed. My car started missing (which I erroneously blamed on the altitude), and by the time I drove into Leadville, at 10,188 feet, the snow was beginning to come heavily. I pulled into one of the local cafes for coffee and information about the river. The radio behind the counter was on and the weather report was grim. I could well get socked in for several days, days which I didn't have. I asked the waitress if she knew where the Arkansas really began. She said she didn't know exactly, but she thought at nearby Turquoise Lake (which turned out not to be correct). She suggested that, with the weather like it was, I wouldn't be clever to try going up there now. I agreed, silently resolving to come back when the weather warmed. I turned about and made it out of the mountains, but already the mystery of the river's source and the incredible beauty of the Rockies and the upper valley had me.

My first brief reconnaissance already was revealing certain special characteristics of this long American river. The very direction of its flow—west to east—makes it interesting. The Mississippi, flowing from north to south, has more of a sameness about it than does the Arkansas, especially the great stretches of the lower Mississippi. Moving laterally across the country, the Arkansas cuts across vastly different terrains. Beginning around Leadville, the trees and herbaceous plants along the river, even to a casual observer, differ considerably from those of the grasslands of eastern Colorado and Kansas. That there are lots of trees is the most obvious difference, but above treeline, in the upper valley, there are plants and animals unique to alpine communities. The most superficial look at the grasslands reveals sagebrush and mesquite that stand in stark contrast to the spruce and pine and the lush mountain meadows.

The rapidity of the change is particularly striking. From Garden City, Kansas, one could go hundreds of miles to the north or to the south and see less variation than in the few miles between Salida or Cañon City and Pueblo. The chief reason for this is the great uplift we call the Rockies. It's not just the fact of the uplifting, the height, but also the conditions that uplifting creates. The winds from the west and north drop most of their moisture as snow, and after they make it over the Front Range there isn't a lot left for Denver or Pueblo.

After several hundred miles across the grasslands, one finally comes to a land of water. By the time one is east of Wichita, or on a line with Tulsa, water comes pouring in, sometimes more than anybody wants. The rains, which here may add up to forty-five inches a year (contrasting with fourteen inches annually for some of the grasslands), funnel into the north-south flowing rivers of eastern Kansas and Oklahoma, which in turn flow into the Arkansas in eastern Oklahoma. The river's character changes radically. I initially considered calling this book *The*

MARSH MARIGOLD · 7 ·

CHEYENNE BOTTOMS

Arkansas: A Story of Three Rivers, for this is almost what one experiences. The white-water stream falling more than a mile in just a hundred and fifty miles; the slow, sand river of the grasslands; and the wide, "full grown" river of the hardwood forests of eastern Oklahoma and Arkansas.

But the more I came to know the river, the more I came to see it as one vast community, though an immensely varied one. What happens upstream often has important effects downstream in this unavoidable unity. At the same time, I was reminded in special ways that the Arkansas River community is not an entity unto itself. To see the dark red flowers of king's crown on Mt. Arkansas after last seeing them above the Arctic Circle, then to walk in Cheyenne Bottoms and see the little Baird's sandpiper that I've seen in Canada, knowing that it's on its way to Argentina, brings this home dramatically and demands that the Arkansas River be understood as part of a much wider world.

I quickly discovered what a large subject the Arkansas River was, and its vastness soon guided me, in humility, toward a somewhat restricted focus. I decided to pursue principally the *natural* Arkansas. My photographs, in the main, reflect a river of contrasting natural communities. Yet the story of the river cannot be told without including man: how he has drunk from it, used it, channeled it, poisoned it, dammed it. The Arkansas has been the scene of much American history that is in the domain of the trans-Mississippi west. Though I begin my story where the river begins, moving as it moves to its end, from west to east, the flow of exploration and settlement (or "re-settlement" by Anglo-Americans) was from the opposite direction.

Rivers of all kinds have been highways to the west. Even if they flowed in the "wrong" direction. Thomas Nuttall, the intrepid biologist of the early nineteenth century, began at the mouth of this river and traveled up through Arkansas and Oklahoma. The Santa Fe Trail picked up the river at Great Bend, Kansas, and went with it all the way to La Junta, Colorado. The miners who struck gold around Leadville and Cripple Creek had also come from the east. If one were writing Anglo-American history as it occurred on the Arkansas River, the mouth, or the east, would be the proper starting place. But I will leave such a history to a justly endowed Arkansas River institute, for such a work would surely take several volumes.

The human story told here mostly reflects how the river appeared to earlier Americans, what they saw and did to the river, and what contemporary Americans are doing to and on the river, what it means to them. Prior to history there was, of course, an Arkansas River, but obviously we know little about how it was or who lived on it. That the river was important to people before its recorded history is clear, and there are a few inferences we can make about those earlier Americans and their relationship with it. The people of the pictographs and petroglyphs in the grasslands, the people of the famous Spiro Mounds, and the Osage and Quapaw, surely knew this river more intimately than we do. The river's water, its riverine world of plants and animals, its smooth passage through the wilderness, combined to make it central to the lives of those who knew it. Spiro Mounds was no doubt a great trade center because of its strategic location on the river, and its proximity to other rivers. The Quapaw in Arkansas lived along

A QUIET BACKWATER IN ARKANSAS

the river because of its many uses. Those uses, then and now, will certainly be part of the subject of this book, as will what modern uses have done to alter the river. This matter is inextricably bound up with science and technology and this too will come up for some examination. While the intentions of the Quapaw and Spiro people may have been the same as those of the miners, irrigators, and tow boat owners, the results of their uses of the river have not been the same.

One becomes a little reticent in speaking about any local section of the river before those who have grown up on the banks of that section—observing it, using it, living by it, sometimes for seventy or eighty years. When Paul Bentrup in Deerfield, Kansas, talks about ditch irrigation, I am at best passing on this talk to the reader. Yet I am pleased to think that there may be some things said about the river in Colorado or Kansas that people in Oklahoma or Arkansas may be interested in and, conversely, Oklahomans and Arkansans may delight in the alpine and grassland plants and animals. For Americans, and for people outside our borders, this book may help to make the river better known, and others may want to come and see it for themselves.

Some of the Arkansas' sister rivers have had considerable literary attention—I am thinking especially about the Mississippi, the Colorado, and the Missouri. Other much shorter, less historically significant rivers than the Arkansas have also received a lot of notice. It has, therefore, seemed necessary, even compelling, to bring the Arkansas into her proper place in the pantheon of American rivers. As Clyde Davis pointed out in the only other book on the entire Arkansas, published nearly a half-century ago, the drainage basin is 185,00 square miles, which is more than the upper Mississippi! Some of its major tributaries, like the Cimarron and the Canadian rivers, are major in themselves, with their own romance and historical importance.

A third of this book deals with the Rocky Mountain portion of the Arkansas, which reflects only a tenth of the river's length; this is a consequence of the book's focus on the broad, natural divisions, or communities, of the river. In the pages that follow, eastern Colorado appears together with Kansas, and eastern Oklahoma appears with Arkansas. There is no question that additional subdivisions in the flora and fauna would be instructive. My primary hope for the book, though, is that it will extend our awareness of what a national treasure the Arkansas River is and, as a result, help us to care for it more deeply.

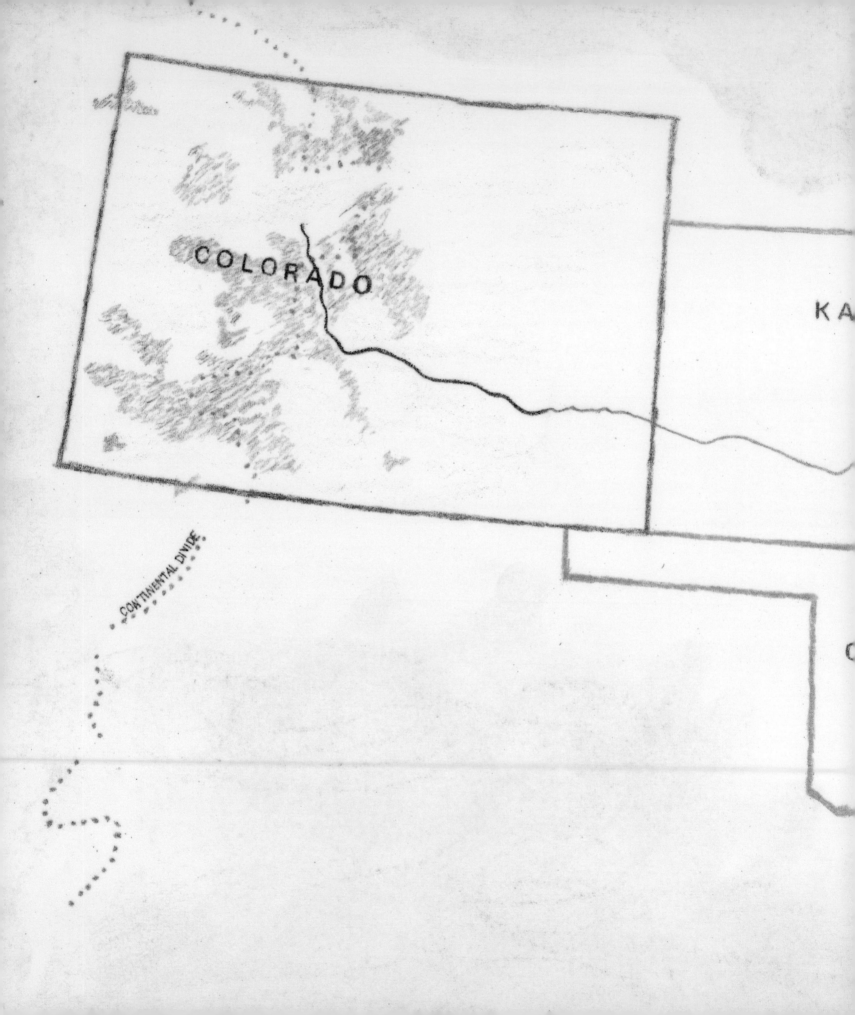

High Country
River

SAS

LAHOMA

ARKANSAS

THE SOURCE

IT was late June when next I drove into the mining town of Leadville, Colorado, anxious to arrive at the headwaters of the river, with the vague unstated notion that only then would I really begin to understand the river. Maybe this is foolish; maybe it's just a Western man's notion that only if he can get at the initial cause of something can he ever be content in his knowledge. But in the beginning this seemed to be the case.

I dumped my things in a motel room, feeling lucky to get one because the main street was crowded with tourists and residents. I had come armed with better maps this time, so I headed north out of town on State Highway 91, toward Fremont Pass. Very soon I could see the clear, small stream not far from the road, and the occasional fisherman snapping his rod and line in a graceful arc, pursuing the tao of fly fishing.

The road began to climb. Before a sudden swing to the left and the final steep slope to the pass, my forestry map showed a turnoff onto what was labeled a primitive forestry road. There the gravel road quickly forked. The left fork led to a metal gate of the Climax Molybdenum Mine, whose offices could be seen squatting near the top of Fremont Pass. No one was to be seen to ask permission for entrance, and there was no mining activity. I learned later that the mine has been shut down since 1986 when it could no longer compete on the world market. So I took the road less traveled by, which soon disappeared around the side of a mountain whereupon one drove slowly near the bottom of a great valley, the Arkansas disappearing far ahead.

After a time I came to a pickup with a small camper on it, parked before a *No Trespassing* sign. I got out, but I could rouse no one in the truck and saw no one nearby. The gate's lock was unsnapped. I thought about the sign and thought about how far I had come to reach the headwaters. Desire got the better of me. Around the very next bend I saw a tall man, standing there, with a pistol that looked a foot and a half long strapped to his side. Standing next to him was a woman; neither of them was saying anything. Nothing to do but keep walking straight ahead. It was too late to turn back. I introduced myself, told them about my project, and fairly soon concluded I was not to be shot.

Someone yelled "Dad?" from down below and soon a pretty blonde teenager came up breathlessly, showing her father some rock she had found. This was the Trammell family from Colorado Springs. They had a mining claim passed down from the previous generation. They were cleaning and shoring up the old mine shaft that the man's father had worked. Far across the valley, about midway up, was a very small hole with some rock debris showing just below it. All this through binoculars. The man, who wore a brace around one leg, had just come from working up there since dawn with his wife and daughter. Quite a trek in any case, but with an injured leg it would be a real chore.

I walked back to the iron gate with them, and he brought out of the truck a picture of his dad working this claim a half-century ago. I steered the conversation back to the beginning of the Arkansas River. He said he had never been all the way down the valley, but that it would be a long hike. I asked him if it was all right with him if I walked down the road beyond the gate and he said sure, but that it ran out very shortly. If I encountered any trouble, I should just say he had let me through. There's a character with a claim on the same side of the valley who thinks he owns it all. There had been rumors of his taking pot shots at trespassers, but likely as not he was shooting up in the air.

I could see that might put an edge on my trip. I showed my new acquaintance the forestry map that revealed a primitive trail winding its way up the slope and then on to Mt. Arkansas. He studied it for a minute and said, "There it is." Just to the right of my car was what I thought was a dry stream bed. He grinned. "Don't think I would try it in a car," he said. "It'll take at least a four-wheel drive. I don't have it on my truck and I wouldn't try it."

I thanked them and said I would try to rent a vehicle in Leadville. I left them standing with their backs against the Mosquito Range, looking like distinctive pieces of Americana. They and the whole town of Leadville evoked the mining past of this part of Colorado, this part of the Arkansas River. It was a past that I didn't know much about. Interestingly, my inquiries about renting a vehicle in Leadville, or getting someone to drive me, led to something called the Mining Gallery. Leadville residents had recommended Joe Swyers, for they knew him as the owner of Alpenglow, an excursion service that took tourists through the mining district or to view the sunrise or sunset in the mountains (thus "Alpen Glow"). Passing through the museum-like exhibits of old mine paraphernalia and examples of various ores, I was directed to a small office where a tall, slim fellow sat. He wore a trail vest and had a broad-brim western hat still on his head. After listening to what I needed, he pulled out a topographical map from a pile and began trying to figure out where the forestry trail was.

"I've never been up there," he said. "It may well be on private land, even though there's a forestry road. A mining claim or something."

"Think we might try in the morning?"

"Best I can promise right now is this: if I don't have a tour booked, and I won't know until late, we can go exploring and just see what turns up."

Luck was running with me this time. The next day the sun was just making its way over Mt. Democrat (14,142 feet) as we left the valley and started up the rocky forestry trail. Joe's vehicle had big tires and a high axle, but even so we had to get out and move rocks that had fallen since the winter thaw. The sheer drop-off and the loose stone had me imagining the nonstop roll perhaps 500, then later, 1,000, feet below. Joe didn't show any concern, but I noticed that every rock and rut had his undivided attention. Especially as the trail hair-pinned and switched back so that we had to back up until our tailgate was hanging over the edge (sometimes hidden by shrub willows), just so we could make the turn. The double dashed line of the "primitive trail" on the topo seemed a little pretentious now.

Finally we climbed as high as we were going to climb. The road broke out of the last Engelmann's spruce and we were above timberline. Before us stretched a long tundra meadow that curved out of sight at least a mile away. From now on we would be in this special world of

UPPER ARKANSAS IN WINTER

the alpine, which resembled nothing else on the river. Russian gets the word *tundra* through the Lapp word *tundar*, that place where the subsoil is always frozen; we get it from the Russian.

My first experience with tundra had come in Churchill, Canada. There, like where I am now, it's where tundra and trees meet. Around the Churchill area, if you go in one direction you may find yourself in *taiga*, (another Russian word, meaning the coniferous patches of forest), and you can observe birds and animals found principally there; or you may find yourself in treeless tundra. That was where I had spent weeks observing and photographing the polar bear. Still I wasn't far away from trees. Later, when I was in Eskimo Point, farther up the Hudson Bay coast, I went out with some natives checking on their trap line and felt the overwhelming power of no tree in any direction until the earth bent under the sky, something that only one who has grown up among trees could feel. I experienced this as a loneliness, being without trees, sensing how much a treed world shapes our human vision in it—limiting our sight, driving our sight upward to the sky, creating mystery with the growing darkness of the forest. An Eskimo, who had once visited a forest, told me he didn't want to live there because he couldn't see far enough. Gods of the forests are different from gods of the tundra. Forest gods may disappear more readily. On the tundra, I suspect the spirits are omnipresent and may be called forth more quickly by human sacrilege or by sacrifice. There are fewer gods where there are no trees; monotheism is a product of the treeless deserts.

One would have to be a stone not to live with a sense of mystery in this beautiful tundra meadow, framed by the great hall of the mountain valley. We moved on silently until we came to a swift brook that rushed over rocks and under a planked bridge that would have to be repaired before we could go farther. Marsh marigolds were everywhere along the brook and made our labor of moving rocks and readjusting timbers much lighter. These brilliant white flowers are in the buttercup family and look more like buttercups than marigolds. To keep their precise identities straight one must use their Latin names. The yellow "marsh marigold" (*Caltha palustris*) is one I was familiar with from knocking around Alaska and the Canadian arctic. The leaves of *C. palustris* I knew to be poisonous; they must be boiled several times if they are to be used as potherbs. I didn't know if this were true of the white species (*Caltha leptosepala*). Instead of eating a leaf, I chose to take a drink from the brook. Not many places in America would I do this, but I was rewarded with what seemed to be the lightest white wine in the world, and teethchattering cold. Good.

Joe decided we had made what repairs we could and should now run the risk of crossing the bridge. We were just a few miles from the highway, but it would still have been an ordeal to get stuck here, hoof it back to town, and get another vehicle to pull us out. We had to work with the few old planks that had been brought in either by the forest service or, more likely, by a miner. While I called directions and Joe steered with the hand of a dentist on his drill, we eased across and were much relieved.

It was not far down the rocky trail that we came to a very wet place, and this time there was no bridge. "We better hike on in from here," Joe said. "I could drive around it, but I'd be

A YOUNG ARKANSAS AMONG MARSH MARIGOLDS · 19 ·

cutting up the tundra . . . and you know all about that scene." As we had filled each other in a bit on our backgrounds, Joe had informed me he had graduated in forestry at Pennsylvania before moving out here. He wanted the high country while he worked on his master's in ecology at the small college in Leadville and ran Alpenglow. Likewise, I had told him about some of my arctic travels.

Growth is very, very slow in alpine-arctic terrain. In this part of the Arkansas valley the growing season is at best three months (it's even shorter in the arctic). After nine months of cold, there is a summer surge of nature's energy, as if the flowers and animals have heard T. S. Eliot's barkeep—"Hurry up please it's time."

Should one walk on or, worse, drive across rocks covered with lichens, it may take a thousand years for the tracks to be covered. For example, the map lichen grows three-eighths of an inch in diameter every thousand years! Even flowering plants may take from one hundred to five hundred years to recoup. Since Joe makes his living taking people on tours, he is particularly conscious of the problem. In my most cynical moments I think Japan's exportation of millions of off-road three-wheelers is some secret strategy to get back at us. From the air in the Alaskan and Canadian arctic, you can see long parallel lines stretching for miles, as if some sky devil had scratched his fingers across the earth. I have trouble imagining the Japanese permitting such violence on Mt. Fujiyama.

At least since Von Humboldt's time in the late eighteenth century we've known that climbing in altitude, whether in the temperate or tropical zones, bears a relation to "climbing" in latitude. This has now been formulated so that one hundred meters in altitude is equivalent to moving up one degree of latitude. One runs into similar communities of plants at certain altitudes that are met by going proportionately away from the equator. Yet, there are some significant differences in arctic and alpine environments. The marsh marigold growing on the shores of the Beaufort Sea above the Arctic Circle has twenty-four hours of sunlight, while this clearly is not the case here in the southern Rockies. Furthermore, the air is clearer and the solar radiation more intense where we now walk. There is twice as much ultraviolet radiation here as there is at the other end of the river, and there is less oxygen. Which I am beginning to feel already as we hike along the trail. Not only am I not acclimated to the altitude, but I am packing about twenty-five pounds of camera and gear. Not in a backpack, but with one shoulder strap of my camera bag. I can see that I may rue this.

Right now, though, there is only exulting in the clear air. The outlines of the visible seem to pop out so that you can simply see more clearly. The tops of the sedges and flowers dazzle in the Colorado sun. Whether one can see beyond the surfaces may be another matter, but many who have experienced life in the higher altitudes think so. Nietzsche felt that all great ideas came from the higher elevations. And the majority of history's mystics were always walking off to the mountains or to the dry air of the deserts.

While the source of the Arkansas River was yet around the bending valley, and my anticipation was building right along, still on the way were many delights too remarkable to be neglected.

TUNDRA DAMAGED BY ALL-TERRAIN VEHICLES

FLAGGED TREES OF KRUMMHOLZ

As one would expect above tree limit, there are no trees as such, but there are shrubs that had they been in the subalpine world would have been trees. Instead they are twisted, stunted shrubs named *krummholz*, the German word meaning *elfin timber* or *crooked wood*. These tortured-looking shapes started out as seeds in the lee of a boulder. With this as protection from the howling, desiccating winds of winter, they take root and begin to make their way. As the branches extend themselves, they create a shelter for others to get their start. Sometimes these shrubs extend themselves high enough to look like a strange tree, with all its branches on the leeward side. All the others have been worn down by the grinding ice crystals and sand particles swept along with the wind. This gnarled, stunted spruce reminded me of some wizened Oriental sage who hadn't been content to live in the lowlands. The important point, though, was that it was there.

"You've hit the flowers at a good time," Joe remarked, as we were surrounded by a sea of yellows, reds, and whites. "We've been needing some rain for weeks and last week we got our wish. Just a couple of weeks ago I was up in the high passes and nothing much was going on. Then, boom."

Plant reproductive strategy in the alpine part of the Arkansas River differs significantly from that of the hardwood forests of the lower river. All but *one* of the several hundred alpine flowering plants in this area are perennials. That is, they do not try to complete their entire life cycle in a single year like the annuals. Theirs is a very conservative approach to survival. Each year a little more is invested, as much as the warmth of summer will permit. If there is a bad summer, there is not much progress, but life goes on. The buds may be just below ground or right at ground level, and if the conditions are suddenly ripe, growth goes forward. It's not a country for speculators, at least as far as plants are concerned.

The only annual in the whole alpine region of the Colorado Rockies is a familiar one from the arctic, a buckwheat called *koenigia*. In the arctic it may be fifteen centimeters high, but here, Joe says, it is only a couple of centimeters high. While wandering in high passes one day last summer he had run into Beatrice Willard, one of the leading authorities on alpine flora and coauthor, along with Ann Zwinger, of *Land Above the Trees: A Guide to American Alpine Tundra*. She was leading a small group of students on a field trip and Joe introduced himself. She was in the process of identifying specimens of koenigia at that moment. Joe promised to take me to the spot this month so that I could see this diminutive plant that has become a sort of star by being one of a kind.

While Joe kept his eye peeled for the off chance of seeing koenigia, we stopped to admire the pink flowers of the very low-lying cushion plant of moss campion. This is a classic example of alpine adaptation, demonstrating in particular a couple of tactics. The first is the quintessential one of keeping a low profile and not asking for trouble from the abrasive wind. Normally the plant is not more than several inches high. Another is the slow growth just mentioned. Put the assets into a strong root system, get good and anchored. Many years may pass

MOSS CAMPION

before even the first few flowers appear, but once rooted moss campion is around to stay. Unless there's some catastrophe like a rock slide—or worse, all-terrain vehicles. Still, its growth rate of a few inches in twenty or thirty years seems speedy compared to that of a map lichen.

Onward. After another twenty minutes of hiking we came to the last part of the valley bend and could see some mining debris from long ago. Then I found what I had been seeking. There at the end of the mountain hall rose Mt. Arkansas at 13,795 feet. In the foreground was the meadow, scattered with points of colors as if Seurat had had a hand in it. The green slope was broken with granite outcrops and, finally, green no longer, the tawny fellfield at the ridge, still with its mantle of snowpack. Joe and I broke out in grins and started our final climb.

On our left the Arkansas ran next to Mt. Buckskin and actually was out of sight to our immediate left, under snow. But above this, as we drew higher, the snowmelt was creating marshy ground as it bubbled past the granite. Suddenly there were so many things to see I knew I must stop, sit down, and begin taking this more slowly. I leaned over and drank from the source. After Joe did the same, he said he was going to climb a switchback to the old mine high up on a southern slope that ridged in to Buckskin. Then we were both alone. And I don't know of anything more important than being silent before such a world.

Where I sat on a flat rock I saw yellow alpine avens and snow buttercup. The buttercup was coming right out of the snow. Around the corner of the boulder was white alpine lily. This was the only member of its genus native to the continent. Talk about a native American. Down the way was an old friend, the deep crimson of roseroot, or king's crown. The last time I had seen this was on Herschel Island in the Beaufort Sea. The leaves and young shoots are eaten raw or boiled by the Eskimo. The leaves of the sedum are succulent, another tactic in the overall strategy of alpine plants. Being succulent helps solve the water problem for these plants exposed to persistent drying winds, or surviving on rocky, dry soils.

Many alpine plants have an abundance of a class of water-soluble pigments called anthocyanin, which include those that give red and purple flowers their colors. Not only the obvious deep reds of king's crown, but yellow flowers often tinged with red, or orange flowers. Anthocyanin is made from carbohydrates stored during the winter below ground. The pigment converts light directly into heat and thus helps to warm the plant tissues when temperatures are still relatively low.

I began picking my way through the strands of brook, climbing toward the place where the snowpack was solid and where I might find the one strand that could be called the Arkansas River's single source. All around me were patches of thick snow. At one place the river fell in a small waterfall and above that was a single stream bank covered with flowers. I stood across it, legs spread, urged by some foolish notion of straddling the Arkansas River in this, the only place I would ever be able to do it. Some kind of comic Colossus of Arkansas. Even so, I sensed some power from it.

I came to realize that my search would lead only to an approximation, as perhaps all search for sources must. Somewhere in the snowpack was a beginning, but maybe never a single point

MT. ARKANSAS

SNOW BUTTERCUP

ROSEROOT

on some Cartesian scheme of things, only somewhere within. Like the incipiency or latency of the origin of a crystal, there to be found under the right conditions. Perhaps I might as well look for the source of the river in the rain and snow as it fell on Mt. Arkansas.

I walked back to the waterfall and ate my one candy bar. Joe was just a speck up the side of the slope, headed to what looked like the mine entrance. Stopping on a boulder pile I looked to the east and into what seemed like a great amphitheater for mountain spirits. Not a place to have small thoughts, or a place where a man could feel in charge of the wild world.

I had had good maps to help me find what I had been looking for, and a perfect day to find it. This was not the case for the first explorers. When I read the journals and diaries of their explorations before the present century, I never cease to be awed by the hardships they endured. Zebulon Pike's story is certainly testament to this. Pike is given credit for discovering the source of the Arkansas, though he apparently did not come quite this far. As a matter of fact, he thought for awhile he had found the source of the Red River, which he was also looking for. During the first part of December, 1806, he and his party thought they had already found the last of the Arkansas below Cañon City, before the river enters Royal Gorge. He struck out north, thinking he was on a Spanish trace that would lead him eventually to the Red River. Finally he crossed over the Mosquito Range and around Buena Vista, thought he was on the Red, ultimately to discover his error. Somewhere between Buena Vista and Leadville, on December 22, he writes: "Marched up thirteen miles, to a large point of the mountain from whence we had a view at least 35 miles, to where the river entered the mountains, it being at that place not more than ten or fifteen feet wide, and properly speaking, only a *brook*." Three days later it was Christmas and the following is most of that day's entry.

Here I must take the liberty of observing that in this situation, the hardships and privations we underwent, were on this day brought more fully to our mind, Having been accustomed to some degree of relaxation, and extra enjoyments; but here 88 miles from the frontiers of our country, in the most inclement season of the year; not one person clothed for the winter, many without blankets, (having been obliged to cut them up for socks, &c.) and now laying down at night on the snow or wet ground; one side burning whilst the other was pierced with the cold wind: this was in part the situation of the party whilst some were endeavoring to make a miserable substitute of raw buffalo hide for shoes &c. I will not speak of diet, as I conceive that to be beneath the serious consideration of a man on a voyage of such nature. . . . Caught a bird of a new species, having made a trap for him.

Someone has surmised that Pike had caught a Carolina parakeet, now extinct.

Nearly four decades later, in 1845, in good summer weather like I have today and with Pike's maps, John Charles Fremont (thus Fremont Pass), leading his third expedition, came to this very place.

Crossing various forks of the river, we finally, on September 2d, reached and continued up the main branch, having on our right the naked rock ridge of the mountain, and encamped at night on the headwaters of the Arkansas in Mexican territory; in latitude 39° 20' 38", longitude 106° 27' 15".

This was pleasant traveling. The weather now was delightful and the country beautiful. Fresh and green, aspen groves and pine woods and clear rushing water, cool streams sparkling over rocky beds.

In a pine grove at the head of the river we came to our delighted surprise upon a small herd of buffalo, which were enjoying themselves in the shade and fresh grass and water. It was now very rare that these animals were found so far west, and this made for us a most pleasant and welcome incident, as it was long now since we had parted from the buffalo.

Some things have changed, some have remained the same as in Fremont's picture. While not Mexican territory, the traveling is still pleasant, and the country beautiful. Right below Fremont Pass the Climax Molybdenum Mine dominates the scene. At the Climax, the river is seized and channeled into a ditch that runs alongside the road. Fremont was very surprised to see the buffalo this far from their normal range; I couldn't expect to see them at all.

As the snowmelt first finds its way down Mt. Arkansas, it is not beginning from the steep western side of the Mosquito Range, but rather from the cirque where I sit, that faces the range, looking east, the way it will flow for most of its length. It goes eastward for the briefest moment, before coming up against the Mosquitoes—here, namely Mt. Democrat and Mt. Buckskin—and then of all things is sent north, then northwest, before doubling back through Leadville and its southward journey down the upper Arkansas valley between the Sawatch and Mosquito ranges.

Although similar geological processes are taking place everywhere (*e.g.*, plate shifting, water flow, erosion), it is easier for many of us to sense their extent and power while standing before fourteen-thousand-foot peaks or one-hundred-mile-an-hour alpine winds. During the Tertiary period (roughly between sixty million and five million years ago), the Mosquito and Sawatch ranges (like the rest of the Rockies) were thrust upward, ever so slowly. Here one is always confronted with how to grasp such periods of time. How does one *feel* the difference in a thousand years, a million years? Are we forced to the abstractions of arithmetic entirely? Perhaps so. We are left with the indefiniteness of "a very long time." We are left with our imaginations as we try to picture a day in the life of a trilobite or a tyrannosaur.

Joe, who is much more used to the thin air of thirteen thousand feet than I am, has begun making his way down the switchback from the mine shaft. But I have all I need to look at and photograph right around me. What I have in front of me at the moment is a large patch of pink snow. It's pink because there are algae growing in the narrow zone as snow passes to its watery state. The algae are reddish or pink, but they are not red algae; rather, they are green algae with a pinkish coat, which brings one back to anthocyanin again. Thus the momentous passage to life for this "primitive" plant is helped along the way by the pigment's capacity for changing light into heat.

Suddenly I see Joe freeze, then drop down, lift his binoculars, and begin to glass some boulders. I don't see anything from this far away, but I can tell by his concentration that something is there. He motions me over. As I pull up to him behind a boulder, he whispers "marmot." I look where he points and locate the small mammal sunning on a lichen-covered stone. I screw on my 300 mm lens and make a couple of shots, but I'm too far away. I crawl along the ground with camera out front, hoping to get within range.

I can't tell the sex, but assume it must be a female, because there is just one male with numerous females in his harem. No way to tell, though. She's light brown, with a lighter band across the nose. Nearly two feet long, weighing maybe ten pounds. I really want a picture if I can get one, because the yellow-bellied marmot, along with some other small mammals in this region, is only found around this part of the Arkansas River. As I ease from behind another boulder, she raises up and looks squarely at me. I am afraid to move anything, but still I want the picture. I move like molasses and fire off one shot, when she gives a shrill whistle and ducks into a hole. I motion to Joe that I am going to stay put, pointing at my watch and indicating twenty or thirty minutes. He nods and eases off toward his own adventures.

All around the burrow there are little trails to other burrow holes, though from here I cannot see the one she disappeared into behind the boulder. These marmots are vegetarians that feed on the forbs surrounding the rock piles. Each adult seems always to have several holes that go to the home burrow, although, if they should be far enough away from this while they are feeding, they will duck into the first burrow they can find. This one wasn't feeding though, so I guess she was home. I didn't know how long it might take for her to pop back up, or if she would do so at all. Near the boulder where she disappeared was a gorgeous stand of Colorado's state flower, the blue columbine.

Not only are marmots special to this end of the river, they are special in another way. They are the largest mammals that go into deep hibernation. Hibernation is understood imprecisely by the general public, and it is not fully understood by those scientists who study the matter. The so-called hibernation of bears, for example, is not the absolutely reactionless sleep that guarantees safety for intruders, as some who have stumbled onto bears in this condition can tell you. Bears maintain almost their normal temperature.

Consider what remarkable creatures hibernators are. Not only are they able as warm-blooded animals to maintain their body temperature surrounded by temperatures lower or higher than their body's, which itself represents a great advance over the so-called "cold-blooded" animals, who are much more prisoners of changes in the seasons, the weather. Hibernators are further able to abandon this remarkable strategy and let their body temperature drop from an average normal temperature, similar to that of humans, down to almost freezing. If we are plunged into icy winter waters, we die from the lowered body temperature. The deep hibernator, like the yellow-bellied marmot, drops its heart beat from around eighty per minute to four or five per minute, and respiration from twenty-five or thirty per minute to not more than one per minute. All of this is marvelous enough, but numerous times during the winter the process is reversed, a process at least as important as dropping into hibernation. The marmot will arouse, then return to the deep condition.

Why did certain animals become hibernators? Possibly it was to escape maintaining high temperature during periods of scarcity of food and perhaps water. It would be one way of

· 32 ·   BLUE COLUMBINE

answering the question Nature put to marmots and every other creature: how will you survive and maintain your kind?

Equally unknown is how the process is initiated by the animals, and how they return to "warm-bloodedness." It is apparently not simply waiting until cold weather comes along. The marmots before me have been busy eating as many forbs as they could, storing fat; and the weather is quite warm, relative to the deep cold of winter. If they waited until it was cold to acquire the stored fat, without which they could not live in hibernation, it would be too late. Some may begin hibernation in mid-August, much before really low ambient temperatures.

Several "trigger" substances have been advanced that could bring on hibernation. Furthermore some of these substances have been extracted from hibernating animals and injected into other species, and have succeeded in inducing hibernation. And what initiates or triggers the trigger? Could it be, as some have argued, that there is a kind of annual rhythm that sets the biological clock of the marmot? For the moment we are left with the many unanswered questions.

At the corner of my eye I realize with dismay that the disappearing marmot has been watching me from another entrance tunnel. As I bring my camera up she ducks. I had waited thirty minutes and missed. I walked over to the big hole where she had last appeared and photographed the blue columbines instead. In a moment I spied Joe coming down a nearby slope. I told him about my miss and he told me that two mule deer had stared at him, the buck finally getting nervous enough to bolt and the doe following behind.

"I guess you need to head back?"

"Guess I have to check whether I have a late evening tour. Hate to go, though. I don't get out just to roam around as much as I used to before the business. Got to figure some way around that," he said.

I was wistful as we turned our backs on Mt. Arkansas, but it was with some satisfaction, too. It's still a bit strange why the finding of a river's beginning should seem to matter. What is also passing strange is that there are many who never pursue such things. Never mind about that, though, on a day like this. I knew now why gods seemed to want to be up in such heights, or at least why so many folks come here to find them.

Again Joe held his hand in front of me so I would stop, then pointed to some small boulders. I thought maybe he had seen some more marmots, but I couldn't make out anything. Then part of a rock moved. Ptarmigan! I didn't even know they were here. What followed was the inevitable rushing and bubbling that any photographer goes through when he's got (and he always does) the wrong lens. Just minutes ago I had been five inches away from some blue columbines.

Still trying to get my 300 mm screwed in, I moved closer, right behind Joe. The ptarmigan wouldn't fly and part of the reason was seen in what soon followed: a half dozen chicks, trying their best to do what their mother was telling them, but still in disarray. What I marvel at still is the perfect camouflage she had in her summer plumage, down to the yellow and brown lichen-covered rock.

WHITE-TAILED PTARMIGAN MOTHER AND CHICK

CAMOUFLAGED WHITE-TAILED PTARMIGAN

She let me get fairly close, but the chicks gave out little "cheeping" calls and she would answer with "alert calls," which served to put the whole family in an anxious state. Finally a couple of the chicks broke and ran across the snow and their mother followed posthaste. It was remarkable how visible they were then, and how they surely must keep to the grassy areas to avoid predators.

I did the best I could with the running shots. Joe and I were both in a state of jubilation about our good luck. "This is only the second time I've seen ptarmigan since I've been up in these mountains," Joe exclaimed.

This was the white-tailed ptarmigan, and the only ptarmigan to breed in the lower United States, much less on the Arkansas River. I knew the ptarmigan from Canada and Alaska, but those were the rock and the willow species. All three have the feathered feet that help them so much during winter. Thus the genus name, *Lagopous*—*lagos* meaning hare, *pous* meaning foot. Besides insulation, this creates a kind of snowshoe for foraging in the drifts. These birds also undergo several molts as a part of their survival strategy. What this female here exhibited was her summer, or pre-nuptial, plumage. Joe tells me that the male during this same time is whiter on the back, thus making him more noticeable during the time of mating and egg-laying. I don't know if there has been any research confirming that more males die from predation during this period or not, but research has shown that the willow and rock ptarmigan males are taken more by predators. They end up being sacrificed for the common good. Males remain near the female until the eggs, which require about twenty-two days to incubate, are hatched. Thereafter the female seems to be on her own, depending for her survival on the buds and twigs of the alpine willow.

Like the survival of most species in the twentieth century, the ptarmigan depends on habitat, and in this case a very specific one. It is not found in Colorado unless there is alpine willow, for its diet consists principally of the buds and twigs of that species.

The last time I had photographed ptarmigan I was with some Eskimo boys who were helping me find nests out of Eskimo Point. We discovered a female on one. I clicked away, getting closer and closer, and still she did not move. Finally I crouched right in front of her and was trying to find her in my viewfinder when she exploded off the nest right at my face. I fell over backwards, much to the hilarity of the Eskimo boys.

With today's mother ptarmigan on her way with her brood, Joe and I resumed our own trek back down the valley, charged now with this experience, neither of us believing our good fortune. Some of the satisfaction was from seeing many things for the first time. Another part of it came from seeing members of the same family, whether of the ptarmigan, or king's crown, or marsh marigold. I knew that this river odyssey was launched in earnest, and launched under felicitous omens.

From the snows of Mt. Arkansas, the river falls some three thousand feet as it arrives on the western flank of Leadville. Just fifteen years from the time Fremont mapped the beginning of this valley, miners hit gold in a place called California Gulch. And placer mining is rumored to have produced up to ten million dollars (of course, these were 1860 dollars) worth of gold. Figures like these are obviously hard to come by because men were often secretive about these matters. By 1870 this strike had played out, and there was little activity until silver was struck in 1877. For the next few years Leadville became the silver capital of the world. From the pristine times of Fremont to the middle of the silver boom, according to one newspaper, the town had picked up "120 saloons, 110 beer gardens, 118 gambling halls, and 35 whorehouses." The mines started petering out around the early 1890s and the town quieted down a good bit. The Climax Molybdenum Mine was a big part of the economy until last year, but there is just enough mining going on now for Leadville to legitimately be called a mining town. But the mining of tourists is more lucrative.

California Gulch, however, is still in the news. The story begins back in the gold and silver mining days. In the first strike the gold miners left cut-over land, ten miles of gravel heaps, and a steady source of mud to enter the river. Then the silver miners left many miles of tunnels. In order to solve the underground water problem, the Yak Tunnel was finished around 1906, and miles of mine water started draining into California Gulch and then into the Arkansas. In 1953 the federal government constructed the Leadville Drainage Tunnel and it, too, drained into the river.

One of the biggest troublemakers in the metal contamination of water is pyrite (or iron sulfide), which produces great amounts of sulfuric acid and iron ions. As this is dumped into the Arkansas the pH goes up, decreasing the acidity and causing a precipitate of iron hydroxide. Sometimes called "yellow boy," this is quite visible. On February 23, 1983, a wooden retaining wall collapsed in Yak Tunnel, pouring disastrous quantities of contaminates into the river. A pumping station forty miles downstream that diverts drinking water to Colorado Springs had to be shut down. After a great outcry, a visit from Colorado Republican Congressman Ken Kramer to the EPA in Denver brought about a study of the problem. The first segment of the study has been completed.

Most heavy metal contamination of the river is not so obvious. Acceptable metal levels established by the U.S. Public Health Service allow a maximum of 300 micrograms of iron per liter for drinking water; 700 micrograms is detrimental to fish. In California Gulch itself, there are 45,000 micrograms of iron per liter. That's a ton a day. There are 60,000 micrograms of zinc, 30,000 micrograms of manganese. Very high levels of copper, cadmium, and lead are present. The effects are not as easy to see as "yellow boy," but they are there. Below where California Gulch enters the Arkansas River, I would not bother to go fishing, because I wouldn't catch anything (and I certainly would not drink from it as I did on Mt. Arkansas). In what fish I might catch farther downstream, stunted growth would offset the heaviness of the flesh caused by heavy metals. Among farmers who irrigate from these waters, there is evidence

CLEAR GRIT MINE

of foaling and growth problems in horses. Horses seem to be more radically affected than cattle or sheep. Stephen Voynick, who has written about hard-rock mining, and specifically about mine metal contamination, has remarked that "metal mine drainage pollution is a national heritage, sort of a deferred payment for the reckless glories of frontier mining."

Don Seppi, an environmental official for Lake County, has an upbeat attitude about the problem, although he explains that merely getting Superfund approval for something doesn't solve the problems. Many people are under the impression that once the money is paid out that's the end of it, but the U.S. government can then turn around and sue all of the individual property owners to get the money back, even though they may have acquired the land after the damage was done. Seppi says that if the miners, with their expertise, can work with the environmentalists and people from EPA, the problems can be solved more cheaply than the cost of litigation.

As I mentioned, water is being pumped to Colorado Springs from the Arkansas River valley. This is one of the curious situations encountered in these mountains. The cities are situated where there is little water. How is it that Colorado Springs can be permitted to take water from the Arkansas valley, which is outside its city limits? Here one enters the nether world of Colorado water rights where water law is based on what is known as the Doctrine of Prior Appropriation or the First-in-Time, First-in-Right Doctrine. Colorado is the only state that uses this doctrine exclusively. The notion of the law originated during the gold rush days when miners had to divert water to wash gold. As new miners came upon the scene and needed water, conflicts arose. The resolution of these conflicts became formalized in water law that established water as a separate property right. Most eastern states have what is known as the Riparian Doctrine. The use of the river is given to those who live along its banks. Many states employ a combination of these doctrines. But in Colorado, water rights (just like mineral rights) can be sold separately from the land. Thus, if Colorado Springs wants to buy the water rights from several mountain ranges over and can afford to get the water back home, it can do so.

By the time one travels past Leadville and Buena Vista, if he is irrigating or fishing or rafting, he may well be using water from west of the Sawatch Range or beyond. Transmountain diversion of water has become a way of life for the big population centers of the Front Range. They could not exist at anywhere near their current population levels if they could not buy the water from the central and western parts of the state. Naturally this sometimes puts them in conflict with the less heavily populated and less wealthy counties—those with less political clout. Residents sometimes complain that sudden releases of transmountain water wash out stream banks and also that the brown trout spawn is ruined. On the other hand, there is more water in the Arkansas than there might normally be.

The subject of the scarcity of water is very much on most people's minds from the beginning of the Arkansas to at least the one hundredth meridian in Kansas. Land with no water or water rights is worth far, far less than land with them. When anything so fundamental and valuable is in question, there is often much conflict. Water law is a specialty in western states. One rural resident told me that if he thought his water rights were being infringed upon, he would have to pay an attorney; and if matters got complicated, he would have to keep on paying. Only those with money can afford to pursue such matters. Large municipalities and large corporations have the wherewithal to pursue the legal side of water rights, as well as the capital to fund large water projects. I asked one Leadville resident if he foresaw any large rewriting of the water law further down the line and he shook his head. "I don't think so. The present law is working too well for the big cities as it is."

———

Although no match for gold mining, another use of the river that is bringing in big bucks nowadays is that made by the commercial rafting companies. They pretty much get a free ride as far as water rights are concerned. From Leadville to Granite the river is not normally floated. From Granite almost to Buena Vista the river is essentially used for kayaking only— although I heard stories about one expert from out of state who had gone down in a canoe. I assume it was a covered canoe. There have even been hardy souls who have attempted rafting this stretch, but kayakers in Leadville tell me it's really not rafting water. In fact it's quite dangerous. It is in this section that the famous "One Through Six" rapids test the mettle of kayakers in numerous races, which include national championships.

But from Buena Vista all the way to Cañon City, rafting companies have set up offices. My experience with one of them left me feeling somewhat ambivalent. At some forty or fifty dollars per person for a four- or five-hour trip, with up to eight people per raft, "there's gold in them thar hills." Some companies are no doubt better than others, though it's not always easy to find out which the better ones are.

An interesting part of the river that is hidden from the road is Brown's Canyon. I wanted to go down it, so I arranged to make camp at the take-out point at Heckla Junction, which is at the end of a rural road between Buena Vista and Salida. I had been warned by Doug Wheat in his *Floater's Guide to Colorado* that during the top of the season the river would be filled with commercial rafters. Since I generally go by canoe or skiff in the lower parts of the river, I did not own a raft or kayak. There was no alternative for me but to go by commercial raft. I had called the rafting company a few days earlier and asked when there might be light traffic, and was assured that the coming Thursday would be the best day. I shared my assumption that the "guides" (the people who row the rafts) were familiar with the geology along the way and was assured that this was so.

My wife Bev and I made camp on a hillside at Heckla in the afternoon. We had for the time being outrun the rain in the eastern part of the state. There was not a single other tent to be seen. Being alone in such a fine place, with the river roaring down the canyon, was perfect. The white birdcage evening primrose seemed to unfold everywhere as the light decreased. As we

BIRDCAGE EVENING PRIMROSE · 41 ·

A YOUNG PINE GROSBEAK

HECLA JUNCTION, BROWN'S CANYON

cooked supper, and breakfast the following morning, young grosbeaks made steady returns to some food my wife had put out for them. She would remain by the river, fishing for trout, while I came down by raft.

Sure enough, there were only two rafts going out—seven people, plus the oarsman, in ours—until we got to the put-in! Then it turned into a baptism on the Ganges. This was in fact a slow day for the particular company I was with, but not so for many other companies who had lined up the motels, gift shops, and restaurants for referrals.

As we were waiting for earlier companies to launch I asked the guy in charge of our boat whether we'd be seeing mostly granite throughout the canyon. He looked as if I had asked him something unseemly and then yelled over to the other raft boss, "Hey, what kind of rocks we got in the canyon?" This was my first clue to how the morning was going to go. The other guy was a little more senior, more sun-burnt, your basic cool river rat; he (who incidentally was from New York City) wore the appropriate Nike nylon shorts. He answered that we would see granite and some sandstone.

I asked one other question shortly after we got underway and our captain advised me to "hold up my quiz" till he finished this section of the river. I put my "quiz" on permanent hold and tried not to let him spoil the river for me, but undoubtedly my one-point concentration was not skilled enough. I enjoyed seeing the dipper as the bird always amazes me with his talent for walking under the rushing water, feeding on the bottom for various water bugs and beetles and fly larvae. He has specially adapted membranes that cover his nostrils to keep out the water and his eyes to keep out the spray.

We never lost sight of Thursday's armada of rafts fore and aft. Somebody commented about that and was told, "This is nothing. Wait until Saturday." The passengers in our raft were pleasant enough. Two kids around thirteen were enjoying the icy spray, and kept asking when we were going to get to the bad stuff. There were two nice middle-aged women in back of them, one of whom happened to ask where the oarsman was from. It turned out that both were from the same section of the same city in Indiana. They chatted about that for a good part of the trip, the oarsman reticent at first, I think because he felt this blew his cover of Rocky Mountain river rat. But the lady from Indiana wasn't interested in that anyway.

At no time did anyone ask anything about the canyon, about any bird, any animal. What Brown's Canyon was that day (and I suspect on many days) was really like the water slides that are springing up around the country. A place for water thrills and spills. But the water slides have several advantages. For one thing, they are not fronting as a "natural experience," and in the long run are probably safer. The rides are certainly cheaper. I'm not recommending that we turn the river into a place exclusively for nature mystics or natural historians. Part of the excitement is the ride, the journey. But the uniqueness of the experience is lost in this "freeway-ing" of the river. Oddly, the oarsman (he was *not* a guide) was into his second or third season. Maybe he was a jaded soul whose sensibilities had been blunted by tourists seeking synthetic thrills. Like trying to be a five-star restaurant in an American feedlot. But he didn't give me that impression.

KAYAKING BELOW BUENA VISTA

The crowded river is an example, I think, of what Garrett Hardin has described as "the tragedy of the commons." Each raft company owner who does business on this commons, the Arkansas River, is locked into a laissez faire system in which he feels compelled to increase his number of boats without limit, but he does this on what is obviously a finite river. "Ruin is the destination toward which all men rush, each pursuing his own best interest in a society that believes in the freedom of the commons. Freedom in a commons brings ruin to all."

The *Floater's Guide* suggests that one way around this traffic jam is to go very early in the morning or late in the evening. You would need your own equipment for this, but it would be better to have the experience the right way, maybe after you have earned the skills to go down, than to have the uniqueness burgled.

The rocky terrace below the mouth of Brown's Canyon was created like the section of "One Through Six" below Granite. During periods of glaciation, glaciers moved down stream beds of the Sawatch and moved great amounts of debris before them, creating large moraines with two results. The moraines themselves created lakes, like Twin Lakes below Leadville, and at the same time the debris pushed the stream bed of the Arkansas toward the Mosquito Range, which is lower than the Sawatch. Through downcutting, the Arkansas River carved narrow canyons like Brown's. Occasionally the debris dammed the river, and when these dams finally broke loose the force of the water was powerful enough to sweep boulders before it through the canyon and fan them out at the mouth of the canyon.

Like the mountainous sections of Oklahoma and Arkansas, the visible geological history of this part of the river is especially interesting. Great cataclysms occurred over such vast amounts of time, and the record is there in all its magnificence. At one time the Sawatch and Mosquito ranges were part of one broad anticline or arch. There was no Arkansas valley. Then that portion of the arch which is now the valley collapsed along a fault line. Over time, streams poured down from the mountain ranges, part of the arch that remained. This fault line has since become known as the Rio Grande Rift. That this was part of the same trough that the Rio Grande flows down has been a fairly recent discovery. If the surface had stayed as it was, the upper Arkansas would have been part of the Rio Grande.

Some great upheaval took place in the northern Sangre de Cristo Mountains, which forced the Arkansas to the east at presentday Salida. From Salida the road is next to the river, as is the Denver and Rio Grande Western railroad. This drive is one of the most striking stretches on the entire river. One assumes that water will seek the line of least resistance, and it is still something of a mystery what forced the river to cut through the hard rock of what is now called the Arkansas River Canyon, when it seems to have been easier to go down the Wet Mountain Valley. But it apparently did it the hard way and we have the scenery for its trouble.

The river leaves Highway 50 at Parkdale, and it's not long before the final assault on what was a wall of granite, the famous Royal Gorge. The evidence seems to suggest that this upthrusting took place as a final cataclysm in the creation of the Rockies. It has also been the scene of great violence during the Royal Gorge railroad war. There are many accounts of that squabble and I won't go into the story here, but the Santa Fe railroad compromised and backed off; the Denver and Rio Grande Western won and is still running freight through the gorge right on up to Leadville. The night Bev and I camped at Heckla Junction, we were startled awake as the earth began to shake and a great, rumbling noise filled the canyon. Still half asleep, I was trying to get my bearings when suddenly the tent filled with a brilliant light and I prepared to be beamed up to a waiting starship. Once I identified the train, I lay back and listened while the eerie creaks and groans of the boxcars filled Brown's Canyon with disembodied yet creaturely sighs of the infernal regions.

Cañon City can conveniently mark the end of the Rocky Mountain part of the Arkansas River. It is still beautiful, and canoeable, east of Cañon City all the way to the Pueblo Reservoir. Incidentally, one of the most distinctive landmarks in Cañon City is the Holy Cross Abbey, a Benedictine monastery that was completed in 1926. Most of the land belonging to the abbey is farmed. It serves as an example of coherent farm practice wherein the land is not considered merely a food factory, but is integral to a vision of stewardship.

One of Cañon City's many other distinctions is that it is the backdrop for a CERCLA lawsuit (Comprehensive Environmental Response, Compensation and Liability Act, which tells us why people prefer the shorthand of the Superfund lawsuit). The Colorado Department of Health has brought suit against the Cotter Mining Company, a uranium processor that, it alleges, has contaminated the groundwater in the subdivision of Lincoln Park. Private well owners have been advised to stop using their wells.

———

The summer of the year following my trek up Mt. Arkansas, Bev and I returned to the upper valley. She was once again prepared to molest the rainbow trout, and we both knew the wildflowers would be at their peak during this late June and early July trip. We pitched camp between Halfmoon Creek and Mt. Elbert campgrounds near Emerald Lake, to be in hiking distance of Emerald Lake so that if I were away from the campsite during the day with the car, she could be fishing. We weren't in a designated fee camping area, mostly because we like to be by ourselves. Our site had plenty of lodgepole pines, and we overlooked Halfmoon Creek, maybe fifty feet below, finding its swift way down to the Arkansas. There was even enough firewood left from the previous fire so that all I had to do was unwind and watch the steaks broil on the grill. We must have been around eleven thousand feet, and the temperature dropped rapidly after sunset. One would not have to be a studied voluptuary to know that this was one of

MULLEIN, NEAR ROYAL GORGE · 49 ·

the peak experiences that the old earth has to offer, cooking by a fire with a rushing mountain stream at campside. This was the second of July, a date I would not have noticed except for the following experience.

The next day I spent prowling around Hagarman Pass and Bev stayed at Emerald Lake. By late afternoon, as I wound my way up the road to Mt. Elbert, I found myself in a dusty stream of cars, trucks, and motorhomes. When I got to the tent, my wife informed me that Friday was the holiday people had before Saturday, the fourth of July! Fantastic. Folks got their three-wheelers and trail bikes unloaded, and until dark they proceeded to make test runs up and down the road to check the open mufflers. The map shows this to be the Mt. Massive Wilderness. I never found out what the deal was: if the road was not a part of it, or if it's ok to freewheel like this. The next morning we broke camp and I went into Leadville to commiserate with my old buddy Joe Swyers.

Over victuals in the Rose Cafe on Harrison Street, he listened to me moan, and chided me for not remembering my country's Independence Day. I told him that was truly a slipup but that I wanted to be independent myself and celebrate in my own way—not by wiping dust from three-wheelers off my bacon and eggs in the morning.

"Tell you what I'm gonna do," he grinned. "You park your car over at my place and load up all the camping stuff in the jeep. I'll take you to my secret place. You can't get there with what you've got, and I have to get back to town and help all these people celebrate. I'll just drop you off and come get you when this holiday blows over."

Done. But I had to promise not to tell where it was.

Being dropped off where there was no quick way out called for bringing the essentials, all of which completely filled Joe's vehicle. The July pattern of afternoon showers offered a distinct possibility of getting wet and staying wet when the sun went down. We'd be there until the weekend was over and most people had to return to work. As we were leaving town, motorhomes streamed down Harrison Street. In Oro City, a replica of a mining camp with mining demonstrations, a crowd was gathering. The residents were putting on a fireworks demonstration the next night.

After we turned off the main road, we bumped along a sagey-looking part of the valley, in which the western blue flag lily was even more startling as it sprang up near a small stream. This flower had been named by Thomas Nuttall, but not in these parts. Nor was he on the Arkansas River when he named it, but the Missouri, as the Latin name (*Iris missouriensis*) tells us. Although this one is considerably smaller than the irises along the lower river, it's a happy surprise to find it here at all. Knowing that it was named by Nuttall is another thread in the web of the river system. Nuttall thought he was going to make it to the Rockies, but he made it only to Oklahoma where illness forced him to turn back. Yet this lily serves as his representative.

As we got into the brief foothills, there is a sprinkling of piñon pines. I especially like to smell the smoke of a campfire of piñon. It brings back good memories of New Mexico and Arizona (rafting along the Rio Grande near Taos, for example). Once at the Bodhi Tree Book-

WESTERN BLUE FLAG LILY · 51 ·

store in Los Angeles, I found incense made of piñon and bought a load of it just so I could recall archaeological digs I had been on, or fishing trips above Santa Fe.

Soon Joe turned off to the left on another of what the maps call, affectionately, a "primitive road." If you knew in advance there was to be a road there, then there was a road. As we started our very steep climb the piñon disappeared and the lodgepole pine came into its own, to be mingled with Douglas fir a little higher. The trail was not very solid and loose gravel occasionally streamed below, emphasizing the height we were quickly gaining—and making Bev a little uncomfortable, though she wasn't saying anything. She is very stoic or Indian about showing fear and pain. Sometimes it is only long after an experience that I find out how she felt about it.

We must have climbed a thousand feet and the understory of the woods was very clean. Like a movie forest. I remarked about this to Joe, asking if it had been control-burned, but he didn't know. There was little moisture here; a local biologist referred to it as a green desert. It didn't even get the snow that the higher elevations got.

Still we climbed. After maybe another five hundred feet we lost the lodgepole and Douglas fir and were now in scattered Englemann spruce. We passed some very old remains of a couple of mining cabins, just a few logs near the bottom left. Except for the occasional dynamite, this life must have been as silent as it was hard. This wasn't a place like California Gulch in the boom times. Just a solitary claim, with a heap of tin cans left outside the door.

Joe said nothing to prepare us as we climbed the gentle slope from the deserted cabins. The world suddenly enlarged itself in a small jewel of a lake, but as soon as the sides of the bowl ascended there were no more trees. We were appropriately speechless and knew already what a gift he had given us.

We unloaded near some big boulders by the lake's edge, but away from the trees. Although during the day the tent might get hot, we didn't want to be next to a tall spruce in a lightning storm. With our pile of gear dumped in a heap around us, I shook hands with Joe.

"See you in a couple of days," he smiled, and was soon bumping down the trail to the valley far below.

When his vehicle could no longer be heard, Bev and I both felt the delicious solitariness of our circumstance. But soon we fell to making camp, organizing ourselves in this great silence. It is at such times that one feels part of a very long camp-making past, thousands of years. Surely this is one of the oldest rituals. The neolithic camper didn't have a choice and we do, but left here, we have chosen to have no choice either. So get on with preparations.

It wasn't long before Bev had water boiling for coffee, for she never travels (if she can help it) without her Community Coffee, made in her native Louisiana and now a gourmet choice in the fancy food magazines. The same battered drip pot has accompanied her to the hotels of New York and Los Angeles. She doesn't like coffee you can read a newspaper through. Not long after her first cup, she had her fishing tackle out. She fishes only with live bait, and salmon eggs

BIG-ROOTED SPRINGBEAUTY

Rather than moving upslope for the present, I drifted back the way Joe had taken. Not far from the miners' cabins were some brilliant scarlet paintbrushes, my third figwort in the last thirty minutes. The bracts, or modified leaves, just below the flower are equally as bright. Although species of paintbrushes will change, paintbrushes will be found in parts of all the states the Arkansas flows through—just one of many links of commonality.

Down a little nearer to one of the cabins I heard some chittering. I took out my pocket binoculars and glassed the area. Soon a little light brown head popped up from a hole and looked in my direction. I had taken a seat by a rock; maybe he didn't see me. I decided to take it easy and watch what happened. Before long, not the one I had first seen, but another came loping along, then stopped and sat upright. A Wyoming ground squirrel! People hereabouts call them picket pins because of the way they snap upright when they sit. I don't know if the other one had given some signal or if the second one was just checking on his own. Apparently I had not alarmed him enough because he went about his business of eating the herbs in the neighborhood. Soon number three came scampering along a well-worn narrow path. None of them joined up with another; each was feeding alone. Number two disappears for a bit, but when she returns two young come scampering not far behind. They are half her size.

The young are not feeding close beside their mother, but are only a few feet away. After a while number three moves in a sidelong path that puts it near the little family. The mother stops eating and sits up as number three edges several steps closer. Immediately the mother begins chasing her out of the area.

The young can't be more than five or six weeks old, or so I would guess. They spend the first four weeks below ground, which means these little fellows are just getting to know their neighborhood. They are soon nibbling on the stems of grass and herbs, a pretty quick transition to make from weeks below depending upon their mother's milk. They were born blind and hairless. They have just a couple of months to reach their prehibernation weight as the mother must reach hers, before the long sleep underground.

Abruptly, clouds begin to pass in front of the sun and I start to lose light. It sounds very commonplace, but the outdoor photographer depends wholly on sunlight; his work day comes quickly to a dead end if he is not lucky with the light. I look over my shoulder and see a deep gray mass moving from the west, over the Sawatch Mountains and headed our way. I start back up the trail, stopping now and then to examine some flowers. While I am squatting for a moment, I look over at a small boulder. There on the top a golden-mantled ground squirrel sits, apparently not very frightened. His colors are much prettier to human eyes (and presumably, to other golden-mantled squirrels) than are those of the Wyoming's. There seems to be a mantle of reddish brown about his head and shoulders, and his entire coat is shinier than the other's. He lets me take off my macro lens and put on a longer one. *Snap*.

The wind is picking up rapidly and there are small waves on the lake. I tussle with a tarp I have brought and try to rig it up quickly between two trees. Tying it off is made doubly interesting by the flailing wind. When Bev sees me struggling, she abandons her fishing.

WYOMING GROUND SQUIRREL

GOLDEN-MANTLED GROUND SQUIRREL

Soon the big drops whack the tarp and we try to stay out of their way. At first the wind grew worse, as the line of rain passed over, and I didn't know if the tarp would hold. Soon, though, the rain settled down to a light steady drumming. Close to sundown the light fell rapidly because of the clouds. Hopes for a campfire diminished with the rain, and it became cold. I was soon pumping up the one-burner Coleman to prepare a rainy night meal. A can of hot pork and beans and a can of roast beef on the side. Some thick hard rolls from the Leadville bakery. Not bad. Almost every time I am out like this, eating camp chow, I wonder why even the simplest things taste better. What a price one pays for being cut off from deep sensory experience in the steady state of air-conditioned homes, picking up much of the world from pictures on television.

Shortly, there was a new pot of Community Coffee dripping. As we huddled close to the Coleman and felt ourselves cupped in the great granite bowl left by the Ice Age, it was possible in fleeting moments to think we were the only people. Maybe a little like the small family bands of the first hunters as they trudged down the continent following the great herds.

In our thick down bags we fell asleep listening to the now-gentle rain on the tent fly. During the night I half awoke and thought I heard creatures moving about. One of them that came close to the tent even seemed large. The rain had stopped.

Morning was as pure and crystalline as the first day of the world. It was also just above freezing and I quickly became the wood-gatherer as my contribution to breakfast. To quote a farmer from the lower part of the river, "The man who cuts his own wood gets warm twice." I think he was quoting Henry Ford. Soon the dry needles curled in dense smoke and shortly we had our breakfast fire. While Bev eased into the morning and started the eggs and bacon, I eased through the spruce near the lake's edge. I saw my very first Cassin's finch. It had a brilliant red crown and there was no mistaking it for a rosy finch, which is also in the area. Both nest here. Neither is found in the grasslands or the hardwood bottoms of the lower river.

Some kind of bird moved ever so slightly about head level, but was in the shadows. I got closer and closer, but still it did not fly. A hermit thrush. As I drew within eight or ten feet, it made an annoyed chirp and merely moved around the tree. I followed until it finally disappeared into denser branches. It never flew from the tree. Maybe there was a nest.

After breakfast Bev resumed her research of the rainbow trout and I decided to investigate the talus and boulder fields. To get there I walked through a strip of woods that had undergrowth thicker than usual for conifers. Several had fallen over and a few shrubs had grown up around the fallen trees. I stopped and stared at a small patch of something brownish-gray that you just know by the texture is not plant. I couldn't see anything else. I remained frozen, and soon it moved a little, just enough that I thought maybe it might be a small fawn. Then it disappeared and after a few minutes I walked toward where it had been. At some distance I saw what it was—a snowshoe hare! It really was the biggest I had seen, fat on the lush meadows hereabout. When one is used mostly to eastern cottontails, these hares seem enormous. Their famous feet seem disproportionately long. When the snow comes along, they must seem just about right.

CHIPMUNK

I walked out of the trees and along the base of the fallen rock. There on top of a boulder was a white-crowned sparrow. It nests here, too, but this was getting almost to the end of its southern nesting limit. In my field guide I had noted seeing it around Norton Sound. Nome is on the northern shores of the sound. The little white-crowned nests much farther north, at least all the way to the Beaufort Sea. Come winter, however, and we see it throughout the length of the Arkansas River.

It occurred to me how I sometimes overlook certain birds or plants because I become accustomed to them and the miracles that they are. The bird before me at this moment is the American robin. It nests nearly as far north as the white-crowned sparrow. Because it has been so successful in making a living and reproducing its kind, though, it sometimes fails to get its due. Yet here they are, doing what robins do, between eleven and twelve thousand feet. It reminds me of an ornithologist friend and his ornithologist visitor from Germany. The American had his son take the German out to do some bird-watching. The son was trying to do a good job and thought of a couple of rare birds, or ones out of their range. Instead the German visitor was ecstatic over our cardinals and blue jays. And well he should have been.

Since the army my hearing is not the best, but I thought I kept hearing high-pitched squeaks or whistles. It was hard at first to tell where they were coming from but, at last, after loafing long enough by the rocks, I saw what it was—the pika. He's just a bit of balled fur, but engaging as he can be. He works like crazy. Interestingly, he belongs to the same order as the hares and rabbits: *Lagomorpha*. He's even called a rock rabbit by some. His ears are very short, though, and keep him from looking "rabbit-like." Like the snowshoe hare, but unlike many of the other small mammals up here, this little creature doesn't hibernate. His solution to the long winter is to cut grass during the brief summer and, just like a farmer, let it cure in the sun before he brings it into his den. Otherwise the grass would get moldy. Still, even with the most prudent behavior, rations are scarce, and the little pika, who passes hard and soft fecal pellets, has learned to recycle the soft ones by reingestion.

I left the pikas in peace and picked my way up the cirque. I made my own pattern of switchbacks since the slope was quite steep. No alpine meadow this, just talus and scree. A mine shaft bore right into the center, but people who had been here before had plugged it. Either they wanted no accidents, or they wanted no one else to have it easy when their way had been hard. I had no intention of getting to the top, but just thought I'd let my body tell me when it would prefer to stop. That wasn't long in coming.

Far below, I saw Bev reeling in a fish and knew that all was well in the world of the *pescadores*. Above the trees like this I could see far down the Arkansas River valley. The view would make a fine photograph. Unlike a photograph, though, which stops change, freezes time, all around me was changing. The scree that tumbled below from such a solid looking mountain brought this point home in a palpable way. How astounding to discover that the very valley has been part of a great dome of rock and then slumped thousands of feet to what we have

PIKA

ROCKY MOUNTAIN BEE PLANT

now. Except for volcano eruptions and similar events, change is harder to see in rock. That's probably why the early Greeks came up variously with water, air, fire as the primary substances of the world, substances that readily manifest change. Not that their visions were easy to come by. It is not easy for most of us to persistently avoid the delusion that we and our worlds, at base, are permanent.

Enough meditation for today. That's what thin air and high mountains will do to you. I'll just have to keep following this river to see where it leads me.

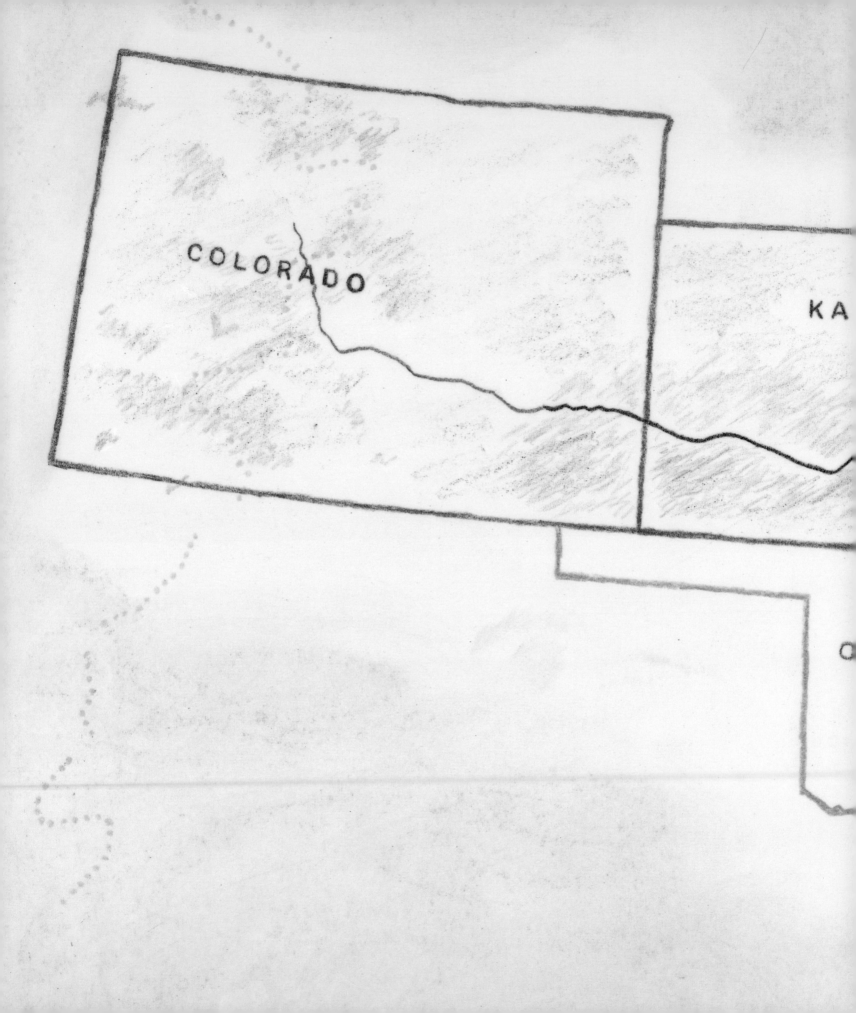

Sand River
Of the Grasslands

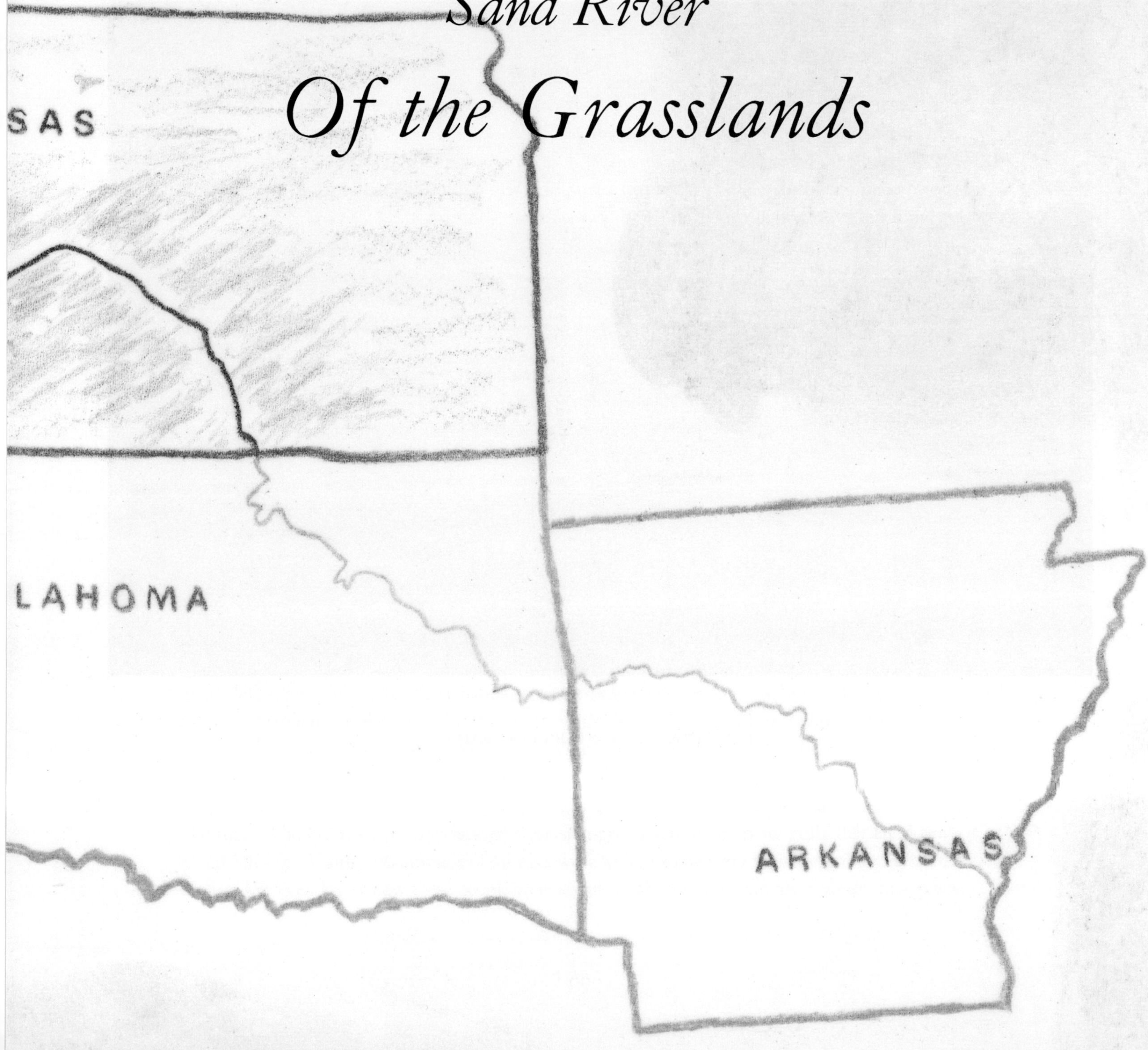

SAS

LAHOMA

ARKANSAS

removed first, then the forelegs and shoulder were removed and stripped of meat, and finally the hind legs were removed. Atop each pile of bones were the skull and vertebrae. Wheat estimated that sixty thousand pounds of meat were cut out. How much was used fresh and how much was cured we don't know.

In addition to informing us about Paleo-Indian butchering and hunting techniques, the chipped flint tools that were found have taught us that such hunting bands wandered considerable distances as they pursued their living, since their tools were demonstrably from other places. It seems clear that other hunters were in the Arkansas valley hundreds of years before this, perhaps even before stone tools were used, but a buffalo bone in the hand is worth two in the dark, and we know what we have on the Big Sandy.

Another leap in the human time scale brings us up to the historical period. East of Pueblo aways the Spanish influence is obvious in the faces of the people who work the farms and in names like Manazanola, La Junta, and Las Animas (although local pronunciations have been Americanized a lot). There has been water in the river that flows by these towns whenever I have passed through, which may seem an odd thing to say, but just over in Kansas the water often disappears. Here, though, one finds lush truck farms, the famous Rocky Ford cantaloupes, and emerald hay fields that produce so many cuttings a year as to make a lower river farmer envious. One reason for this is that irrigation farming is a lot more certain than depending on the rain. The fields get the water when it's needed and not, for example, when the hay is on the ground. Actually, many irrigators don't want rain. They'd rather do it on their own schedule.

One fall day I walked along the Arkansas River west of Lamar, Colorado, with Tom Betts, a local newspaperman. Tom, who seemed to be in his mid-thirties, grew up on this part of the river and had canoed sections of it in eastern Colorado, something we could not do this day because there was almost no water in the river. We had chosen this part of the river to visit because, for one thing, we could see in outline the foundations of New Bent's Fort, constructed in the 1850s by William Bent, one of the famous Bent brothers. The fort held the high ground above the river. This area of the river was part of what was known as "Big Timbers," a forty-five-mile stretch of cottonwoods which, according to Marc Simmons, in *Following the Santa Fe Trail*, was the first significant stand of timber west of Council Grove in Kansas.

The bluffs of sedimentary rock contribute much to the pleasant scenery and also give good vantage for viewing the river and the surrounding country. There are some cottonwoods, though nothing like what was described at Big Timbers. This point on the river is also known as the Amity Headgates, because it is here that one of the numerous long irrigation canals has its beginning. A concrete dam has been thrown across the river and on the northern end of it all the river's waters drop through the headgates to make their long journey watering the fields of wheat, milo, and corn in eastern Colorado and western Kansas. The Amity Canal is, by itself, 110 miles in length.

The water that stops at this dam and enters the headgates is being released from the John Martin Dam, which lies east of Las Animas and west of Lamar. Prior to the building of such

A CLOUD OF RED-WINGED BLACKBIRDS, LAS ANIMAS, CO. · 73 ·

EAST COLORADO IRRIGATION

dams (including the one at Pueblo, and others on tributaries of the Arkansas in Colorado), the spring run-off from snowmelt created a peak flow that culminated in June and July. Since the construction of John Martin in 1943, the water has been stored, and then released to irrigators when they call for it. Tom told me that the current release, which we were witnessing today, was soon to end and winter storage would begin. When released water stops flowing, the level drops to the base of the rock bluffs and petroglyphs or rock carvings can be seen in the caves that have been undercut by the river.

Thus, on one side of the dam and then upstream, the river was quite alive, and looked like a river was "supposed" to look. Below the dam there was nothing. It is a strange sight for a downstream person to see a river stopped in its tracks. This strangeness is repeated some thirty miles to the east when the river begins to flow again . . . from what is left of the return from Amity Canal.

Much of the land north and south of the river is too far away to irrigate, but it wasn't too far away for folks in the late nineteenth century and early twentieth to try and eke out a living, because quarter sections (160 acres) could be homesteaded. It sounded like a good deal back east and many came. The trouble was that 160 acres might be adequate for intensive farming with forty or fifty inches of rain and deep, rich topsoil, but such was not the case out here on the marginal soil of the plains. The grasslands could hold their own with thousands of buffalo grazing on it, and it did fairly well with cattle; but once the grass cover was broken by the plow, the persistent prairie wind did the rest. These two elements came together in the 1930s, contributing to an economic depression for the country and absolute disaster for the prairie farmers.

In the mid-1930s the federal government helped to resettle the failed homesteaders by purchasing the land and placing it under the Soil Conservation Service. Ultimately these acres ended up in the National Forest System and are now known as our National Grasslands. A great number of people in Colorado and Kansas have never heard of the immense areas. Of those who have heard, few have visited them. Yet, to know the High Plains even faintly as it once was, and to know the shortgrass prairie of the Arkansas River valley, one must go there.

A lot of places are called prairie nowadays simply because there are no trees, but true prairie wasn't plowed. Many speculate that not even a hundred years without disturbance would be enough to return the land to its true prairie state. Should you travel along the Arkansas River today, you would mostly see wheat fields, broken up some with corn, hayfields, an occasional feedlot. The essence of the overall modern picture of the Arkansas valley's prairie is the cultivated or grazed field. All this has happened in a mere hundred years. For millions of years before this, the valley was covered with grass.

The part of the Comanche Grasslands closest to the Arkansas River has its northern extremity at La Junta. Here there is an office for the upper part of Comanche called Timpas, after Timpas Creek that cuts a northwest diagonal through it. The Mountain Branch of the Santa Fe Trail ran along Timpas Creek to Trinidad and finally over Raton Pass.

SEDIMENTARY STRATA WEST OF PUEBLO

CENTER PIVOT IRRIGATION, WEST OF LAMAR, CO.

LUBBER GRASSHOPPER

Today the sun was high already and for once the wind was not blowing much. The directions I had received were somewhat general, but this canyon was supposed to be easy to find. I later discovered that my guide had expected me to be able to drive much farther, then get out and walk.

Already the great silence was beginning to do its good work. We came to a few twisted junipers and then some beautiful prickly pear cactuses. Many living things are more striking when they're showing off their sex, and the prickly pears were no exception. Perhaps on another day and in another season, I might have overlooked them. But in this poor soil and rocky terrain their yellows and oranges were suddenly very beautiful. Some were yellow with orange centers.

Cactuses offer good examples of special desert and grassland adaptation. When even the grasses are gone, perhaps from over-grazing, cactuses remain. In the case of over-grazing, the spines of the cactuses no doubt account for their survival. Adjustable pores in their epidermis help them to retain moisture during the dry months; then, in the fall, the pores open so that they get rid of much moisture from the tissues in order not to burst when the frigid arctic air comes swooping down from the north. This is why they look dried out in the fall. Their adaptive strategy over great periods of time has brought about very fleshy stems for water retention, the spines for protection and reduced leaves. Interestingly, two other families quite different in their leafy forms, the milkweed and the spurge, have evolved convergently. Now the three families often look similar, because the same forces urged them to this form. The fruits of the prickly pear, which ripen later in the summer, are great favorites in Mexico.

Our walking had taken us down into an arroyo. It was here that I expected the rock art that Hollenbach had told me about, but as hard as Bev and I scrutinized the walls, nothing turned up. Then we came upon the roofless rock house he had mentioned; and I realized we should have driven farther in.

The walls overlooked the arroyo, and we clambered up to examine it. We were not right on the Santa Fe Trail, but I remembered his saying this was what people thought was a stagecoach station. The only thing passing today was the wind—and maybe an occasional rattlesnake.

The arroyo now turned due south toward the Oklahoma panhandle and the walls were so much higher that the arroyo could be called a canyon. Hollenbach said I should anticipate some vandalism and that I wouldn't have any trouble seeing it, that the place had occasionally been used for target practice. I hadn't realized he meant at the very petroglyphs. Just as the canyon seemed to join another one as it widened, and as the sandstone assumed the windworn sculpture that any artist must scramble to approach, we saw the glyphs. What made them easy to spot was the red spray-painted letters of some cretin's brave expression of lust for his lady friend. The impact of this was increased, I am sure, by the serenity of the quiet canyon, the weather-worn canyon walls, and then, of course, the drawings and the defacement of figures done by someone long ago. I don't know. Maybe the science-fiction writers are right. Maybe the human race was started by some virus, or perhaps some waste dumped off by a space ship a long while back. A former state archaeologist of Colorado has classified such folks as "Vicious Vandals" to distinguish them from the "Commercial Miners," or the mercenary pot-hunters. Next to this defaced figure was a bullet-riddled quadruped of some sort. Hard to tell with so much of the sandstone chipped away. Colorado officials say the defacement of rock art is very prevalent, and there seems little that can be done, especially with available manpower. Jim Hollenbach alone has to look after all phases of activity for the entire Timpas area.

When I later phoned someone in the forest service in Denver to inquire about the areas I was going to write about, the gentleman there asked me not to mention specific places because it would just make matters worse. Being asked as a writer to hold back something makes me uncomfortable, but I concluded that it would be in the public interest not to say specifically where I was. The vandals likely never read books anyway and so would never see this account, but matters are so bad now that even the small risk of more devastation is too much.

A severely beautiful natural counterpoint to this human atrocity was the cliff swallows' nests in the overhanging canyon ledges. Delicately shaped by each pair of birds, mud bit by mud bit carried in their mouths, the nests take five days to build. The elegant cliff swallows had nothing (we think) but utility on their minds, only getting on with reproducing and perpetuating their kind. And in this deepest of all materialism they left something that implicitly, silently ridicules the degenerate side of our species. Later this summer the swallows would be winging with their brood back to South America.

Fortunately, the mud nests were beyond the reach of the vandals, or maybe they had been made too recently for the shooters. I focused on the least damaged of the glyphs and tried to salvage what I could in my responsibility to imagine, to recall the lives of those who'd made them, what they might have been saying to themselves and, in turn, to those who might pass this way. Maybe I would have better luck in another place.

Bev and I planned to camp in the lower part of the Comanche in the evening and knew we'd better head back. In this unfamiliar country, we didn't need to let dark catch us. After we climbed out of the canyon and the arroyo that led to it, we came across a special prairie resident, the ornate box turtle.

Its range is west of the Mississippi, and it favors the open grasslands and sandy soils, unlike eastern box turtles. One day while I accompanied Ken Smith of the Arkansas Natural Heritage Commission on an inspection of the handful of prairie remnants left in Arkansas, he had pointed out one of the special adaptations of this prairie turtle. The eastern box turtle is found along the margins where the prairie meets the trees. When prairies catch fire, or fires are set (which may ensure that the land remains prairie), the eastern box turtle that ventures out beyond the trees is caught by the swift, windblown blaze; in the aftermath many of them can be found in the blackened grass. The ornate box survives such quick-striking calamities by being able to dig very rapidly below the surface. It hibernates, digging down for its winter sleep. On the plains it may take advantage of prairie dog tunnels and save itself the effort of digging. Joe

PRICKLY POPPY

ORNATE BOX TURTLE

Eagleman and John Simmons note in an article on Kansas weather in *Natural Kansas* that "low winter temperatures establish the northern range limits of . . . the ornate box turtle. Since it hibernates underground, the depth to which the ground freezes is very critical for this species. Throughout most of its range, including Kansas, ground freezes to about fifteen inches below the surface. Where ground freezes deeper than thirty inches, ornate box turtles can no longer survive the winter."

Both box turtles have a hinged plastron that is able to snap shut against the carapace and make a protective "box." Unfortunately, this shell does not protect it against trucks and automobiles on the highways where we see large numbers of them dead.

Turtles have been around since the Mesozoic era. Even among the reptiles, theirs is the longest living line. They got it right the first time and have stayed with it. While we're fooling around with the idea of making ourselves extinct, we help others like the ornate box turtle on their way. The road kills are bad enough (Have you ever been in a car with someone who swerves to hit a turtle?), but unfortunately the placid nature and the beautiful shell of the ornate are getting it into worse trouble. These turtles, who have already lost much of their habitat to farming, are now greatly admired by many Europeans and Far Easterners. A booming trade ships thousands of them overseas. The wholesalers have trained bird dogs to sweep fields very rapidly and get perhaps all of them!

This is an example of what has been called "capitalizing nature." It's not enough to look at the ornate box turtle and enjoy his being. He's not even being used as food (which incidentally would be risky business, because these turtles can eat poison mushrooms that don't affect them but that may be passed on to those who eat them). Someone looked at the turtle and saw a profit. If there were no buyers, of course, there wouldn't be any collectors with their bird dogs. Between the cultivating of most of the land and the collecting of the turtles by enthusiasts here and abroad, we may soon have to visit a condo to see this little turtle. The matter is perhaps not as simple as I am making it, though. Our relationship to animals and plants is one of the most perplexing problems that thoughtful people have to face. Having to kill animals for food is much a part of the discussion, and plants are living, too. To say wittily, "I don't eat anything with eyes," as George Bernard Shaw remarked, is just that—a witticism. The shape of sensory receptors should have nothing to do with it, and these remarks are nothing but anthropomorphism of an obvious kind. Such matters bear in a similar way on one's relationship to a river, culminating ultimately in one's relationship to Nature.

On the way out, there were hundreds of cliff swallows along the road, dusting themselves or feeding nearby. Going south on State Highway 109 we crossed Purgatoire River with a thin stream of water in it. Numerous High Plains creeks and arroyos entered the Purgatoire, and it entered the Arkansas at Las Animas. There are many references to it in the diaries of early pioneers. After an hour we were back in the Comanche Grasslands, now the southern section. As we drove, the great vistas took our breath away. On the right day, they might have struck terror in our hearts. I have not yet seen the steppes of Asia, but I suspect that it may be something like this. I can imagine some Russian peasant looking up from scything wheat and seeing a cloud of dust on the horizon, realizing that the horse-riding hordes were on their way again to rape and pillage. For that matter, crossing this land before me a hundred years ago, by horse or wagon on the way to Santa Fe, and suddenly seeing a Kiowa or Comanche silhouetted on a ridge, must have had the same effect.

Our assumption had been that we would get more food and water on the way to our canyon rendezvous, but as we entered the grasslands from the west, Utleyville was the only village on the map, and either it has been abandoned or we missed it, but we soon realized that we wouldn't see any other town. I stopped and got water from a farm hand, who said he had never heard of the canyon. It showed on the forestry map, but (at least to strangers) this was flat, largely unmarked terrain. We felt much as if we were at sea, following instruments and the pure abstraction of the map. We had been off paved roads for some time, and soon we were off the all-weather road. The only point of reference was a pipeline pumping station, and that would guide us only if we had the right pumping station. I vividly remembered a time when I was living in Oklahoma and could not take my customary route because a bridge had been washed out. The rain had turned the normally hard surface into great streams of mud. While I was busy dodging the most obvious holes I lost my sense of direction and there wasn't any sign of the sun in the sky. That land had been laid out just like the land in eastern Colorado, square section by square section, the work of surveyors who had no interest in the aesthetics or eccentricities of bends in the road to break the monotony of straight lines. When I finally found a farm house I realized I had been "squaring" about for a long time, not far from where I had started.

The checkerboard pattern is characteristic of the National Grasslands. The land did not come to the government in one large chunk. It was purchased from failed farmers, often a quarter-section, 160 acres, at a time. One moment one may be on private property and the next on federal land.

Here in southeastern Colorado, with the help of our odometer and by counting sections one mile to a side, we reached the place where we must now leave even these rough roads for the "primitive" roads. A structure was marked on the map at this point; sure enough, the small ranch house remained. The rancher had created a tiny oasis with well water; his brilliant green grass and garden plot offered stark contrast to the surrounding prairie. He answered my questions about what lay before me and in the course of it I admired some of the hounds in his yard and kennels. He said he used them to hunt mountain lions, which were numerous hereabout.

I was happy to know that I would be only a few miles from his ranch if something went wrong. We were still on his land when we turned off the "rural" road to the "primitive." Bev nudged me, for some hundred yards off to the right four pronghorn were standing. They were frozen, but as I wrestled with my camera case and slowed the car, they wheeled and gave us a fleeting example of North America's fastest land animal. Lord, they were moving! As I put the camera's viewfinder clumsily to my eye, all I could make out were four rearends in overdrive. Those white rumps, another example of adaptation, are their "signaling devices" to other pronghorns. Such signaling would largely be lost in the dense hardwood bottoms of the lower Arkansas, but over the great flat distances of the prairie their white flags of warning can be seen farther and move faster than sound can be transmitted. That's why we wouldn't find the pronghorn down in the canyons we would soon come to. There they would be much more vulnerable to mountain lion attacks and hunters. Often called an antelope, the pronghorn is not a member of the antelope family. It is placed somewhere between the goat and the deer; its horns are hollow like a goat's, but they are shed every year like those of a deer.

I was momentarily let down by not getting a picture, but tried to counsel myself as I had done before: the experience itself is more valuable than the picture. That kind of counsel shouldn't be foremost in a photographer's working mind, or he would be out of a job; but he does have to guard against the bad thinking that the only valuable experience is the photographable one. There is no getting around it; concentrating on making a good picture can limit experience. Just to see such elegant, swift runners was reward enough.

The rancher had told us that a number of people, including archaeologists, had been in the canyon, and that we could drive right down it and see most of the petroglyphs. He said that we would eventually come to the Oklahoma-Colorado line and that there were more beyond that, but that we would have to walk a good distance on private land. The driving always assumed going very slow because a car, with its low clearance, is not fitted for this. After what seemed a couple of miles, we even came upon an official sign in front of a great canyon face, urging people not to deface the petroglyphs. There was a single tree in the shelter of the canyon wall. As we pored over portions of the wall, we again found the glyphs and, sadly, the same sort of aggressive destruction of the rock art. I climbed up into a rock shelter and even there people had gone to some effort to deface the figures.

We continued down the canyon, looking for an abandoned stone house. The rancher had said that the area might be a good place to camp and was central to more petroglyphs. As the canyon made a big bend and straightened out we saw the house, looking much like the old stagecoach house back at Timpas. But it was built very close to the west wall of the canyon. Perhaps the two gnarled trees that struggled near it had been planted by the former occupants. Even more striking was a high rock shelter some ten feet from the base of the canyon wall. From our campsite we could see far to the south. Opposite us, across the way, were magnificent rock formations. In the course of my conversation with the rancher, he had alluded to some visitors who were advancing this part of the canyon as a Celtic observatory. Mainstream archaeologists think the notion that it is Celtic is farfetched. There have been a proliferation of sites advanced in recent years as observatories. For some the evidence seems quite strong; for others it's rather tenuous. Obviously, if you get enough points on a plane, whether it be marked by rocks or radiating lines of some sort, several of the points will line up with humanly significant solar or lunar positions. I didn't know what wall of the canyon this presumed observatory was supposed to be on. I did know that we had once again found a great place to camp in an immense landscape within an immense solitude—the kind of solitude that is getting harder and harder to come by in America.

In about a minute we had our four-person nylon tent up. As anyone who has used them will know, four-person tents are for two people, just as two-person tents are for one. Tent craft has become so advanced now that our tent had the shock-corded poles built into the tent fabric. We merely had to connect the ends.

We eagerly struck off across the canyon floor to the opposite wall, perhaps two or three hundred yards away. The craggy heights and several deep fissures seemed to come together in my preconceived idea of an ancient observatory. Bev prudently waited below while I did a little climbing. There was a large hole high up and I thought I might be able to see if any shaft of sunlight might slant through and give some indication of a place of alignment. All I managed to do was get on top of a great balanced rock with no possibility of seeing into the hole. I had a fine view of the canyon, though. The wind was stronger up high and was picking up. Clouds from the southeast were scudding along and I decided to come down, which for a bit was tricky. Not being an accomplished rock climber, I always forget it is sometimes easier to go up, looking at the hand- and footholds, than it is to back down. It is also easy to overestimate one's strength as he tries to lower himself without footholds. But with fool's luck I managed to get down without cracking my head open. I walked through one of the great fissures that reached the ground, the walls being quite black (perhaps from fire), and the wind whipped through with mysterious speed. I saw no glyphs.

We started down the sage-dotted slope and came upon a young cottontail. Bev, who has the good sense to be as excited over a tulip as a tiger, said "Quick, take his picture." I thought the light was too muted because of the increasing clouds, but I hurriedly screwed on the 200 mm lens. I thought the young cottontail would likely be in the next canyon before I could get close enough, but it seemed to have almost no fear. As I peered through the viewfinder I saw a couple of huge ticks, engorged with blood, attached to the rabbit's head. Not your Audubon ideal of a rabbit picture, but a true one nevertheless, revealing a real part of a rabbit's life.

He scooted off and so did we, back to our camp, concerned about the changing weather. I had asked the rancher if there was any danger of flash floods here and he said no. We had set up our little stove and victuals underneath one of the twisted trees, but when the lightning began to fire away several miles down the canyon, I thought the better part of wisdom was to move up into the deep rock shelter behind the abandoned stone house. The trees were after all very good lightning rods. A few drops began to fall and I took the little stove up to the rock shelter because Bev wanted to have her cup of evening coffee.

Here was to be our great surprise and pleasure. On one side of the shelter were two fine petroglyphs. A large one seemed to be a buffalo. There had been some vandalism, but the

YOUNG COTTONTAIL

glyph was mostly intact. Probably some archaeologist had traced the outline with chalk in order to photograph it, and the outlines were quite clear. The back legs were carved so that the animal appeared to have four back legs, but there were just two in front. This figure was below the flat ceiling, but above a very flat ledge where I had placed the stove. Everywhere else was too uneven. The ledge was just right for cooking and there seemed to be shallow metate hollows on the ledge surface for grinding corn. Just below the ledge was a much smaller, but (glory!) unvandalized glyph of a horned animal, this one slighter and with horns like a deer or elk.

We also had here an excellent view of the canyon and we were completely protected from the driving wind. We had not wholly escaped the tree as lightning rod, for *within* the rock shelter, in a fissure that had been struck by a Bunyanesque wedge, a tree had sprung triumphantly, its trunk quite above the top of the shelter. Maybe it was a risk, but it surely seemed a risk worth taking and one that had been worth it for other nomads passing this way.

Bev, the ritual coffee master, began her ceremony, just the right amount of water, the steady hand and eye pouring the loose coffee grounds into the pot with the sureness of a Japanese teamaster, then arranging the waiting cups. Like tea, coffee may keep the mind fresh and vigilant. In a dynamic and beautiful setting such as this, surrounded by the art of those closer to Nature than we probably will ever be, we hope to come to the feelings of the tea ceremony: harmony, reverence, purity, tranquillity. The simplicity of what we were doing, of what we had with us, was absolutely essential to the magic of the evening.

Who were the people who had etched the "buffalo," and the "deer"? I couldn't know this evening and I wouldn't know later, because it is most difficult to date such art. Generally, there is no stratigraphy. One band of people may have come through in A.D. 100 and scratched or pecked out a buffalo, and several hundred years later some other may have added a deer or a shaman. I saw no horse and though this is not conclusive, it may mean that these earlier people came through before "contact," before the Spanish brought the horse in the sixteenth century. Let's say, for the sake of this evening as the lightning sheets and ripples the sky, that this was before the horse. The people who stopped for awhile, or passed through, would have been nomadic hunters and gatherers. Those hunters up the Big Sandy north of the Arkansas likely had much in common with these, in their need for these animals on the wall. There had been some bad times on the plains five to seven thousand years ago (the Altithermal) and the place was hotter and drier than now. Buffalo were scarcer in all likelihood, and certainly water and grass were less plentiful. But the people made it, somehow; maybe by withdrawing to certain fastnesses near the mountains or even farther east. Still they depended on the buffalo, the quintessential plains animal as far as its importance to man is concerned. As far as we know, there is no petroglyph going back to Big Sandy Creek times. Far from it. I think the earliest we have comes around 2000 B.C. But sandstone is a chancy medium. If glyphs are in exposed places, time with its erosion of the world works on such art as well as on mountains. No, this buffalo, this deer, were not of the Sandy Creek time.

PETROGLYPH IN COMANCHE NATIONAL GRASSLANDS

In a canyon nearby some glyphs have been dated about A.D. 100. There are signs that by this time there was some relationship between the people here and those east of the plains. Such evidence is reflected by archaeologists as they designate this culture "Plains Woodland." Somehow contact was made, for much later, after A.D. 500, pottery similar to that of eastern sites showed up. Still there was no horse and still there was much in common with Big Sandy people. Ideas about how people should be treated at death, before they make their great journey, appear to have changed though, as reflected in their burial practices.

Sometime before the conquistadors came with their horses, the people known as the Kiowas, and the Kiowa-Apaches, seem to have left their hunting grounds where present-day Yellowstone National Park is. They moved, or perhaps were pushed, slowly southward until such time as history began to be written of the region south of the Arkansas River and north of the headwaters of the Cimarron. This land was known as Kiowa country. Ancestral Kiowas could have been in this very canyon some time before the conquistadors. Perhaps they spent many nights in this very shelter.

Our current understanding of the meaning of these animal figures is uncertain. Even if one can date them closely, it is difficult to get the figures to speak to us as they spoke to the people then. Ethnographers have used the knowledge of what art has often meant for "primitive" historical peoples to make educated guesses as to what it might have meant for their ancestors.

The animals were of vital importance to the people who carved and pecked these figures into the stone—that seems beyond question. Most of what we know about such people, historical or otherwise, insists that animals and plants were considered to have souls. When the buffalo or the deer was slain, the slaying was serious and had consequences. If the killing was not done with the proper form and handled respectfully, the hunter was in great jeopardy. As I noted in *Bears and Men: A Gathering*, Aua, an Iglulik Eskimo of Hudson Bay, told the explorer Knud Rasmussen, "We fear the souls of dead human beings and of the animals we have killed." Aua's brother added to this that "the greatest peril of life lies in the fact that human food consists entirely of souls." It is not difficult to imagine the tension that the hunter lived under, considering that the plants and animals necessary for his life had to be killed and at the same time their souls had to be propitiated.

Modern man has attempted to short-circuit this polarity, but even now he remains uncertain. Part of his answer has been to have surrogate killers do the job in factories; like so many matters concerning birth and death, we put them out of sight, or fragment them so that they are unrecognizable. The person who carved the figure of this buffalo did not live in such a world, and his art and religion helped him to deal with his world. I am not insisting that modern man cannot kill an animal and think of it as nothing but meat; but unless he is able to maintain an extraordinary egocentricity, he is then haunted by another idea: that *he* is nothing but meat. He may counter the anxiety by creating a religion that tells him the earth has been put here for his exclusive use and that he is the only creature with a soul, yet he remains uneasy.

If the people who carved these figures were of the Late Prehistorical period, as some archaeologists have suggested to me, then the Kiowas who came to control this region for a time would have come upon them as they swept through the land on their horses. The Kiowas were not the only ones to be in this part of the plains and the Arkansas valley. South of the river were the Kiowa-Apache and the Comanche. To the north were the Cheyenne, among others.

The Kiowas were typical Plains Indians, however, and many generalities about them are true of the others. Once the Plains Indians came into the possession of the horse, their story and the story of the land became a different one. It is ironic that the ancient forerunners of these Indians came from the east, across the land bridge to a place where the horse had been, but had become extinct. The horse in the Orient ultimately became domesticated and made its way west, finally to Spain which was responsible for its appearance here in the sixteenth century. The catalytic effect upon the culture was almost as swift as that of the internal combustion engine on the west. While we have yet to know what final effect our machines will have on our world, some, like Mildred Mayhall in *The Kiowas*, see the meteoric rise of the Plains culture brought about by the horse as containing "the seeds of its own deterioration: its predatory characteristics were antisocial and vicious—against other Indians as well as against the white." By 1875, the culture was shattered; the horses were taken away from the Kiowas and the buffalo were essentially gone.

The buffalo was at the center. No story of the Plains and no story of the Arkansas River can be told without reference to this animal, properly called the bison. While both the ornate box turtle and the buffalo can teach us, the buffalo holds a higher profile in history. The sheer magnitude of his numbers and the centrality of the animal to the Plains Indian culture will always make him a symbol of what has been lost. Peter Matthiessen has noted that "the bison herds were almost certainly the greatest animal congregations that ever existed on earth, and the greed and waste which accompanied their annihilation doubtless warrants some sort of superlative also." The Indian was very wasteful of the buffalo and his new "tool," the horse, permitted him to be so, with repercussions that he did not foresee. Yet the Plains world might have had enough elasticity (how forgiving the earth has been of our bungling so far) to permit the waste until the Indian could be instructed by foresight, some inkling that there were limits. Far more repercussive was the coming of the white man with his guns and just as little foresight. An inkling of the necessity for restraint could have been had for the looking by the Europeans. Many of them had come to America because limits and scarcities were already on their homelands. Before the American carnage was over, the world was lucky that there were a handful of these animals left anywhere to be put in reserves and helped toward a modest comeback.

The lesson the buffalo can teach us is a clear one, and it can serve to instruct us in our relation with the river. Certain ways of thinking, certain attitudes that have served men well for millennia in maintaining life may suddenly become self-destructive because the rules have changed. A thousand years ago a small band of people might hunt as hard as possible, might plant as much as possible, and just maintain themselves. The difficulties were enough to impose limits from without. Because the pre-horse Kiowa, and the Quapaw of the lower river, did not feel that they could overpower Nature, they were reverent before the world and lived in relative harmony with it. While many of the limits were imposed from without, there was clear evidence of self-control aimed at perpetuating the natural harmony.

Suddenly the nature of the life game changed as the Kiowa acquired the horse and as Anglo-Americans brought their guns. Later, the Kiowa had guns, which increased the slaughter and ironically gave them more time to make war on other tribes as well as against the invading white men. Soon that part of the Kiowa story came to an end. The invaders from Europe not only kept building better and more lethal weapons, but they also invented tractors that could plow up the whole prairie, leaving little grass unturned. New machinery permitted massive water diversion, whether in Colorado or Kansas. Ultimately the Plains ecosystem or the earth system will bring an end to the story, one way or another. This is why the restraint deriving from a sense of harmony with the world is the only permanent corrective to these sudden changes brought on by quantum jumps in power. We must learn that we aren't obliged to do something merely because it is possible. A simple idea, but one that is difficult to inculcate in the national mind.

The few sprinkles of our early evening shower have long ago stopped. Though the sunlight is gone, the sheet lightning furls across the sky, lighting the entire canyon. I have never seen such persistent lightning. Our lantern continues to flicker, illuminating the buffalo and deer, and as the flame wavers in intensity, the figures almost seem to live. Dramatically, the yip-yip-howl of a coyote up canyon focuses the entire nocturnal landscape, taking us deep within its wildness and deep within ourselves. For a brief moment, all of us—canyon, coyote and we—coalesce.

Lying on my bedroll later in the night, I was in a focus of light in the tent's circle. The on and off of the lightning became some great prairie semaphore, and though I could not sleep, I was not afraid.

One year later, in early June, we entered the Cimarron National Grasslands, adjacent to and east of Comanche, but in Kansas. It is named for another famous tributary of the Arkansas River, the Cimarron, which flows through part of it. This grassland covers 108,000 acres, and the forest service manages twenty-five miles of the Cimarron River as a special riparian wildlife habitat. Much of the time there is no water visible in this part of the Cimarron, but it was an unusual year and there was a flow of water, mostly ankle deep with the occasional hole. Other years you can dig a foot or so down in the dry river and find the water that moves very slowly southeast.

CIMARRON CROSSING IN WINTER

CHOLLA CACTUS

· 100 ·   CHOLLA CACTUS

The cholla cactus, one of the beautiful cactuses in the southwest, is found in southern Kansas and Colorado. Sometimes called the tree cholla, it can be up to seven feet tall, though the ones I saw were between three and four. The deep red of the cholla can take your breath away. Its effect, I think, is so heightened because the cholla appears in landscapes that are often only varying shades of brown; the red flowers and green stems offer beautiful relief. Once the flesh of the cholla has withered away, the inner structure manifests a network pattern that is most interesting. People use it in floral decorations, in furniture making, and even as walking sticks. The curve-billed thrasher usually nests in the fork of the cholla. Perhaps the thorns serve as protection once the nest is built, for they are quite painful to humans. This thrasher eats, among other things, part of its own house, the seeds of the cactus.

The people of the Cimarron grasslands are proud of their population of lesser prairie chickens, and rightly so. The population is diminishing everywhere in its former range, which has been reduced by 55 percent in the past twenty years. It is smaller than the greater prairie chicken (as one might expect) of the tallgrass prairie in the Flint Hills, and its population is smaller.

About five miles after entering the grasslands from the east and fording the normally dry river (I had to get out and walk ahead this year to be sure the car could make it), one comes to a prairie dog town. The black-tailed prairie dog is not a dog at all, but a ground squirrel. He is also a grazing animal, eating mostly the grasses around his burrow, a burrow which incidentally is more elaborate than that of any other rodent. The opening is about six inches in diameter, but the tunnel narrows and then may drop vertically as deep as ten feet. About three feet down is a guard room or "listening room." Farther down, the burrow has a toilet chamber, a food chamber, and a nest chamber. Unlike the Richardson's ground squirrel or the yellow-bellied marmot, the prairie dog does not go into deep hibernation, though he can stay down during heavy snow cover for a long time. One of the delights of being quiet while waiting for the prairie dogs to reappear after ducking below is to have a burrowing owl stroke its small body across the grass a few hundred yards and settle down until we have gone. I must have counted ten such owls in only a couple of hours.

After a quietly exciting time at the prairie dog town, Bev and I headed slowly back south toward Point of Rocks. As vehicles are familiar enough in this part of the grasslands, it is fun to let the car pull itself along quite slowly and watch what turns up along the way. Horned lizards (the so-called horned toad), Great Plains skinks, Cassin's sparrows, long-billed curlews. But a show-stopper for Bev was the black-tailed jackrabbit that raised up twenty feet from our car. There's something oddly humorous about this hare, and no doubt his ears are much a part of the humor. He was nicknamed the "jackass rabbit" because his ears resemble those of that animal; later the name was simply shortened to jackrabbit. Besides contributing to this animal's acute hearing, his long ears radiate heat and thus serve to cool him in the blistering summer weather. His humorous appearance is furthered by the length of his hind legs in comparison to the eastern cottontail. When he needs to, the jackrabbit can cover the ground at up to thirty-five miles an hour. As Vernon Bailey has written, "All they ask of a coyote is a fair start and an open field." He doesn't need running water, which is just as well, given his choice of habitat, for he gets enough from the dew on the grass he eats.

Another inhabitant of the Plains as typical as the jackrabbit is the yucca called soapweed. Its range is quite wide and includes eastern Kansas. During the early part of the summer this plant is in magnificent bloom, loading the upright stalks with its drooping bells of creamy white. Sometimes these stalks can be three or four feet tall. I have heard that some people use the petals in salads, and cattle seem to like them. When they are in grazing land, often every flower is stripped. Jackrabbits rear up to eat the flowers. It gets the name *soapweed* because Indians made soap from it. This yucca depends exclusively on the so-called yucca moths in the genus *Tegeticula* for pollination. The female lays her eggs in the ovary of the flower, and the larvae feed on the seeds. After ovipositing, the female thrusts a mass of yucca pollen into the stigma of the flower in which the eggs are laid. Pollen is then collected by the long curled tentacles on the maxillae. Other yucca moths that lack these tentacles can't pollinate the flower, but their larvae feed on the flower stem and the fleshy part of the fruit.

As our day wound down we arrived at Point of Rocks, a famous landmark on the Santa Fe Trail. It is an excellent vantage point from which to see the winding sand river of the Cimarron and to get a panorama of this part of the Great Plains. The wind soughs persistently, and if you lean against a rock on this little mesa, it doesn't take much imagination to hear the creaking of the wagons as they moved between the base of the bluff and the river.

One is standing on an outcrop of the Ogallala Formation at Point of Rocks. As I have said earlier, this is a great wedge-shaped layer of sand, gravel, and silts deposited during the Tertiary period. Interestingly, there is also an outcropping of the Jurassic, the only such outcrop in Kansas. Much older than the Ogallala, the Jurassic began around 205 million years ago and ended 138 million years ago, long before the present Rockies were formed. But it is the Ogallala that holds great interest for the people in western Kansas nowadays, for it is in these sands and gravel that water has accumulated over millions of years. The formation covers most of the western third of Kansas and parts of seven other states. In some places it is 350 feet thick, but on average it is 100 feet.

The Ogallala reaches just into Colorado from the Kansas line and completely undergirds the Arkansas in western Kansas. The return from irrigation canals like the Amity that began in Colorado creates a persistent flow in extreme western Kansas, for example, in Hamilton County. I wanted to get the feel of the river (where there was a river to get the feel of) and had the good luck to run into Joe Kramer of Kansas Fish and Game. Joe is a wildlife supervisor for the southwest region of Kansas with offices in Dodge City. He is also an avid canoeist, and frequently takes his group of Explorer Scouts on canoe trips. He agreed to a trip from Coolidge, Kansas, to Syracuse.

BLACK-TAILED JACKRABBIT

YUCCA, CIMARRON NATIONAL GRASSLANDS

A WINTER PRAIRIE, WESTERN KANSAS · 105 ·

HORNED TOAD

POINT OF ROCKS, THE CIMARRON RIVER, AN ARKANSAS TRIBUTARY

I rendezvoused with him in Garden City where he took part in the annual buffalo roundup. Men from the southwest district corraled the small herd just south of town and, as they ran each one through the animal "squeeze," blood samples were taken and shots were given to those that needed them. Regular range cattle are no great fanciers of being caught and manhandled in this way, but buffalo especially have no liking for it. Everyone has to make a special effort not to get caught on the ground inside the corral, for these undomesticated animals are unpredictable.

The following morning we put one of Joe's canoes in at the Coolidge bridge. Just two days earlier, a northern front had moved through with rain and freezing temperatures. Although it was below freezing at sunrise, the day soon warmed up and, with the heat from our paddling, we had a fine time on the trip. Joe laughed that if I told folks in Kansas City about canoeing in western Kansas, they likely would scratch their heads in disbelief. Not far to the east of where we were they would be right, for there is essentially no flow in the river from Garden City to Dodge. Now, though, the morning danced on the riffles of an Arkansas that seemed to be moving about three miles an hour. We did not see any human for the next fourteen or fifteen miles.

Joe seems to me to be the completely engaged wildlife professional. Besides leading his Explorers, he is the president of the Kansas chapter of the Wildlife Society, co-chairman of Quail Unlimited, and a member of the Upper Arkansas Water Basin Advisory Committee. I couldn't have had a more appropriate host for this section of the river. Just to start the morning off right a golden eagle wheeled overhead, heading for an old cottonwood some distance downstream.

The plowed fields were actually not far away, but down on the river's surface we were in a corridor of cottonwood, willow, and salt cedar. Beyond the south bank was sand-sagebrush prairie and north of the river was the typical shortgrass prairie that we left in the National Grasslands, mostly buffalo grass and blue grama on unfarmed land. One bright spot on the habitat horizon is the nationwide Conservation Reserve Program that offers farmers money for not planting crops (which has a familiar sound), but they either hold it for ten years in buffalo or blue grama grass, or seed it for the better and taller grasses for wildlife, like bluestem, switch, or side oats grama. This is for highly erodable lands, and the west has plenty of that.

I had the bow while Joe masterfully handled the stern, and when a pheasant cock exploded from one bank and disappeared in the salt cedars on the opposite bank, I was beside myself. Not living around pheasant, I am light years from becoming blasé about them. Against the browns of autumn, the scarlet wattle stands out like a tear of blood. The salt cedar (also called tamarisk) and willow provide good cover not only for the pheasant, but for lots of other small game. It's a veritable oasis compared to the wide open shortgrass prairie. Cottontails can dodge the numerous raptors; and before this day was over, we had startled a whitetail doe from her daylight dozing. She too disappeared in the brush.

There is considerable concern for and research into the riparian habitat in eastern Colorado and western Kansas, partly because of its wildlife support, and because much of this habitat is dying from lack of water. The riparian community has undergone considerable change in historical times. What is sometimes not known is that diaries and other records tell us there were

BUFFALO ROUNDUP

generally no trees along the river. There was the unusual stretch near Lamar, Big Timbers, and isolated spots like Chouteau's Island west of present-day Lakin; but as noted earlier, Council Grove far to the east marked the resumption of trees.

This can be accounted for in several ways. The river bed from bank to bank was much wider before settlement (the 1880s) than the one we canoe down today. Then it was a quarter-mile wide because of an undammed peak flow due to spring run-off. Old pictures from this early time show great sweeping bends in a meandering river and large point bars (sandbars created on the points of a turn in the river), the opposite bank being the bend where the channel was deeper. Any beginning vegetation was swept away in the current and the banks were scoured. Soon after the great surge of water was over the river was greatly reduced, and any remnants of vegetation not swept away died from lack of moisture.

Then the Arkansas valley was settled by farmers, which soon meant ditch irrigation, and the diverted peak discharge gradually caused the river to diminish in width, which in turn permitted encroachment in the old river bed. Through the first sixty years or so of this century, woody vegetation continued to expand its territory. Such expansion not only diminished the width of the channel of the river, but because of the increased soil-holding capacity of the vegetation, caused the river bed to rise, and flooding of the surrounding valley land occurred more frequently. The flooding was abetted by the diminished heights of the river banks that formerly had been created by peak flow.

Suddenly, in the 1970s, the center-pivot well came into being, and the water table began to drop. This is why one sees so many dead cottonwoods today; cottonwoods must have abundant water. Along the banks, one of the last plants to go is the salt cedar. This shrub or small tree was introduced from Asia in the early 1900s and is now found in abundance along western rivers. Not only is it more drought-resistant than cottonwoods, it is also more salt-resistant, and the salinity of the soil and water of the Arkansas valley is increasing. Salt cedar has been a mixed blessing, though. It serves as good wildlife cover and has a high capacity for holding the soil along the bank, but at the same time it uses a lot of water in a country that can't spare any.

Landowners have reputedly cut down cottonwoods along the banks because they, too, use a lot of water. But on this day of canoeing I saw many trees that had been cut down by beavers. A great many. This is about all these animals have to eat along the river. Joe is trying to help matters by trapping beaver during the winter, but it's on his own time. Last year I think he got sixty. That has to be mostly a labor of love, because wintertime on the Arkansas River in Kansas is no joke.

During a sandwich break on a sandbar, we saw slate-colored juncos feeding on the seeds of some kind of thistle that makes up part of the understory of the shrubs. Along with the juncos were song sparrows and the larger Harris and white-crowned sparrows. They ducked for cover as a marsh hawk came lofting over the southern bank of salt cedar and willows, only to be frightened himself by discovering us there on the sand. Before the day was over we must have seen ten of these marsh hawks, in addition to the large ferruginous hawk and the rough-legged hawk. Joe was to remark late in the day that he had seen more raptors on this trip than any previous one. Likely this meant that last year their food supply had been plentiful and the clutches had been large.

On eight or ten occasions we had come upon either gadwalls or mallards, sometimes a single pair, sometimes two pair, as we eased around the gentle bends in this now severely controlled river. They were always off the water and gone before coming into camera range. Yet one unusual drake stayed on the water before us and then of all things hid in the undercut of the bank. Joe declared that something must be the matter, because he had never seen a mallard do that. We paddled upstream as best we could, and as the drake tried to escape, it was clear he was dying right before us. Joe picked him up from the water and examined his body for marks of shot, but nothing showed.

The day ended on a better note. The final felicity for me was seeing my first northern goshawk. He was really a fast, strong flyer. A friend of mine, the poet Dave Smith, wrote a poem about a goshawk, but at the time I read the poem I had never seen one. Joe remarked that if he had to come back as a hawk, he would just as soon be a goshawk, a fierce predator of pheasant, and even of ducks. After seeing him fly, I wouldn't be sorry to come back as one myself.

———

It should come as no surprise that what happens in one part of the aquifer can influence another part, just as what happens up the Arkansas, or such tributaries as the Cimarron, has a dynamic effect downstream. The fact that the National Grasslands result, in part, from farmers failing because of a lack of water merits mention here for the third time. Through the 1930s, irrigating was principally ditch irrigation.

Ditch irrigation began in the early 1870s in Kansas, and really began booming in the 1880s when more than four hundred miles of canals and ditches were built in Garden City on the Arkansas. During the same decade, ditches were dug around Lakin to the west and in a big way at Dodge City to the east, which sits on the one-hundredth meridian. Ditch irrigation requires diverting the flow of water several miles above the land to be irrigated, at the headgates, and then needs a two-to-three foot fall to be effective. We recall that the Arkansas generally falls at about eight feet per mile. Thus the canal can arc its way through the farms and be released through smaller gates at each field. The size of the gate and rate of flow times the length of time go into figuring how many acre-feet of water the owner of a water right gets. (An acre-foot is the volume of water it takes to cover an acre one foot deep.) Right away one can see that this kind of endeavor requires more than individual effort; it demands cooperation. Individuals come together in an irrigation company. Someone known as a "ditch rider" periodically spot checks the users.

KANSAS SUNFLOWER

WILD ROSES IN CENTRAL KANSAS

KANSAS SUNSET

Ditch irrigation had its problems early on, before the aquifers were being pumped. Even by the end of the 1880s, cyclical drought and increased use of the Arkansas resulted in the river going completely dry in western Kansas. If there was little snowmelt and rain for that year, the drain on the system ended up at roughly zero. When the center-pivot pump came into being and proliferated, an entirely new element was put into the equation of the river. The water is pumped from several hundred feet in the aquifer below and is moved very efficiently down a long distribution system which is on wheels. Slowly the whole system revolves around the pivot of the well, leaving a great circle of watered ground. But the water being used is fossil water from the Ogallala. Fossil water is a lot like topsoil. It takes a long time to accumulate, and when it's gone, it's gone.

The people of Colorado and Kansas know that they've got a problem, and there has been some attempt to solve it, but matters already have gone rather far. The Ogallala may replenish itself at the rate of an inch or two a year. In Groundwater Management District No. 3, for example, which spreads across thirteen counties of the Cimarron and Arkansas basins in western Kansas, the overall water level declined almost two feet in one year. The Kansas Water Office has just completed its most comprehensive water report, partly in an effort to predict what the situation will be in fifty or sixty years. In the Cimarron basin, groundwater supplies are expected to drop 79 percent! The Arkansas Basin is expected to drop 49 percent. Gary Baker, the manager of District No. 3, has said that "the state has been over-appropriating water rights and approving too many wells for more than forty years. This isn't an easy job. You might say the horses were out of the barn a long time before we were called in."

What is now being considered as a restraint on irrigation, which accounts for 90 percent of the water used in the Arkansas, is mandatory well-metering, just as in the city. But the aquifers and river basins, and the people using them, are part of a complex web. One portion of the web is struck, and there are repercussions elsewhere. It parallels the problems of water and air pollution. The community downstream doesn't want to face the problem unilaterally, when its upstream neighbors refuse to help. Members of District No. 3 want a comprehensive solution. It's understandable that the irrigators of Kansas don't want to cut back if those in eastern Colorado do not. The solutions to the problems of water rights in these two states have become more difficult because of a dispute that has ended up in the Supreme Court.

In 1949 the two states came together in an Arkansas River compact that would provide operating criteria for the John Martin Reservoir (which is in Colorado) and for a sharing of the water, with Colorado receiving 60 percent and Kansas the remaining 40 percent. Among other charges, Kansas claims that Colorado has appropriated 150,000 acre-feet per year of ground water and that this has directly reduced the usable flow to Kansas. The case will take years, and in the meantime the Arkansas continues to be depleted, perhaps irreversibly.

Some have maintained that economic forces will take care of center-pivot irrigation, either by limiting it, or by causing it to be unfeasible, but if this should have some restraining effect it still would not reverse the depleted aquifer. A rough kind of arithmetic suggests that if the

A DRIED-UP ARKANSAS, PIERCEVILLE, KS.

aquifer is on average being depleted by two feet a year and it replenishes itself at the high figure of two inches a year, then for every year of use it would take twelve years to replenish if all irrigation were to stop. It would take several centuries to get the water level back to where it was.

But why replenish the aquifer? If it goes dry, economic forces will put a stop to it all. Part of the "all," however, would be no flow in the river, which is a condition that already exists much of the time between, say, Deerfield and Dodge City. When the aquifer was at its former optimum level, the Arkansas downcut it in numerous places and this helped to maintain flow.

It's delightful to witness the excitement of folks in places like Garden City when there is water in the river. I was standing on the banks in the summer of 1987 with a photographer from the Garden City *Telegram* as she described what a novelty it was and how people from other places seemed confused when you bragged that there was water in the river. Why wouldn't there be water in a river? One of the irregular regional celebrations is to get in cattle tanks and float downstream when there is the shallowest excuse for a river.

I was visiting with Paul Bentrup, a fine gentleman who farms near Deerfield. As we went about while he moved pipes and checked irrigation gates, he talked about how his family has been on the Arkansas River for most of this century, surviving the Great Depression and a few other droughts in this part of Kansas. He got the idea of having a contest to guess when the Arkansas would eventually make it to the bridge in Pierceville, Kansas, east of Garden City. It hadn't in the last seven years, but the previous year it had made it within a mile or so of the bridge. National Public Radio reported on the contest, during which broadcast Mr. Bentrup sang a song he had composed called "Flow Gently, Sweet Arkansas." Any time I have seen the riverbed at Pierceville it was, alas, being used as a race track for three-wheelers.

Mr. Bentrup also has a deep interest in Santa Fe Trail history, along with many of the people in the Arkansas valley from La Junta, Colorado, to Great Bend, Kansas, where the trail runs next to the river. The Arkansas was a sustainer for the wagon trains, everyone trying to stay close to water for as long as possible. The Santa Fe was twenty years older than the Oregon Trail and, as Simmons points out in *Following the Santa Fe Trail*, ended in Mexico. A merchant, William Becknell, opened it, making the first trip in 1821, and the important saga of the opening of the Trans-Mississippi West finally was brought to an end in 1879 by the completion of the railroad.

The town of Great Bend wasn't around when the wagon trains went through that part of the country. Farther west, Ft. Larned and Ft. Dodge were established to provide soldier escorts for the wagon trains and as bases for offensives against the southern Plains Indians. Ft. Larned is quite a fine restoration and preservation of a military fort of the time, and the first thing that struck me was the absence of a stockade, but I learned that this was actually the rule of the army. There was little danger that the Indians would attack a strong garrison of troops. Near Dodge City began several river crossings, this one known as "Lower Crossing," with perhaps the most famous one being the Cimarron Crossing a few miles to the west. Again, river water

PAUL BENTRUP IRRIGATING HIS KANSAS FIELD

THE BENTRUP SHEEP RANCH

· 122 · A HEAD OF WHEAT, KANSAS

was very much on people's minds. From the Cimarron Cut-Off, or Desert Crossing, lay fifty miles of waterless plains until the wagons came to Middle Springs and Point of Rocks, which we noted in the Cimarron Grasslands. The Cimarron Cut-Off Route was one hundred miles shorter than the Mountain Route—if you made it. Besides the lack of good water holes, there was the much-increased danger of being attacked by Kiowas and Comanches.

It was between Deerfield and Lakin that I followed Paul Bentrup around as he watered his fields. Across a portion of his land the wagon ruts can still be seen. He plans to donate this to the Kearny County Historical Museum.

Near La Junta and the Timpas portion of the Comanche Grasslands is Bent's Old Fort. This was the last place the river touched the Trail before heading toward Raton Pass and Santa Fe. It's a splendid reconstruction and an excellent place to get some feeling for the period. During the summer there are on-going exhibits of numerous crafts (weaving, blacksmithing, etc.) that were practiced during the time. This fort, which contrasts sharply with Ft. Larned, was a private one, owned by traders and merchants, the Bent brothers with others. It has a stockade and is close to our Hollywood version of what forts "should be."

Where the Santa Fe Trail first begins to run alongside the Arkansas River at Great Bend is also the location of Cheyenne Bottoms, a sixty-four-square-mile marsh habitat. Because of its critical location between the nesting and wintering grounds of so many birds, it is one of the most important waterbird areas in what is known as the Central Flyway. Marsh around this part of the plains would be scarce at any time, but especially so now that the country as a whole has lost more than half of its marsh. The presence of the Bottoms in this part of Kansas was occasioned by a subsidence in the earth's surface some one hundred million years ago. While the basin surface has no doubt changed over time, recent core samples support the probability that Cheyenne Bottoms has existed as a wetland for at least 100,000 years.

In historical times the Bottoms has undergone ups and downs. Tradition has it that the Cheyenne Indians had a big showdown with either the Kiowas or Pawnees over the hunting rights in the Bottoms around 1825. Apparently the Cheyenne won. At the end of the nineteenth century some speculators were planning to turn it into a big resort. During dry years the necessary water would be pumped out of the underground Arkansas River, which was only ten feet below the surface. This was obviously before center-pivot time. The speculators went broke. Also about this time a group planned to drain it altogether and plow it. The state of Kansas began acquiring land in the 1940s and 50s in order to create a waterfowl area. During this period, the Bottoms was leased to the air force as a bombing range for a couple of years. This no doubt was a great boom to the waterfowl. Once the state began acquiring land it set about acquiring water rights along several streams, including the Arkansas. Precipitation alone would not maintain the necessary water levels, so water was diverted from the Arkansas at Great Bend to the Bottoms. That was fine until center-pivot irrigation began drastically lowering the water table. Soon, in most years, there was no water to divert.

BENT'S FORT

Kansas is now at some kind of critical turning point as far as Cheyenne Bottoms is concerned. A study has recently been made for Kansas Fish and Game which recommends several options for saving the Bottoms, ranging from a hold-the-line half million dollars to a substantial effort at about five million. At the same time, segments of the Kansas economy are down: wheat's down, oil's down. The outcome is still undecided. It is clear to me that federal money should be allocated to help; the millions of birds that pass through the Bottoms are international and intranational. Ask not for whom the bell tolls.

Over and over, the evidence reminds us that the world is a web and that one action one place in the web moves the whole. One does not need long vision to understand that the Canada goose which nests in Canada, feeds at the Bottoms, and then continues farther south in the winter, is going to be affected by conditions at any point in his migration. Unfortunately, just like center-pivot irrigation, the effects may take a few years to show up, and by then it may be too late.

Consider only the broad lines of the ecosystem at the Bottoms. In the most recent analysis, the food pyramid roughly begins with such an example as the narrow-leaved cattails. Many times the cattails are cussed one and all because they can take over a pond or lake, and they can be a problem at the Bottoms. But the cattail gradually decomposes and becomes food for certain larvae and crayfish, muskrats and marsh moth larvae, and plankton. Further up the pyramid come the shorebirds and ducks, small fish and insects. At the top of the pyramid are mammals like the mink and raccoon, and raptors like the bald eagle, the red-tailed hawk, and the great horned owl.

If anything has come out of ecological studies for the average person, it is that you can't tinker with one element or level of the pyramid without a risk of the whole thing coming down. The ecosystem of the Bottoms is a microcosm of the larger world of North and South American birds, and in this world the Bottoms itself becomes a piece of the pyramid. Sometimes observers note that in pre-irrigation times, the Bottoms still went dry. This is true. But during those thousands of years there were also thousands of other marshes, large and small, that could be used if some had temporarily fallen on hard times. Now that man has entered the scene and so greatly altered the natural process (for example, by plowing up most of the Central Flyway), he has a responsibility to the web that he has been shaking so hard and with such disregard. Such a responsibility should be clear, but one's understanding can't be limited to a concern only for one's front yard or farm: what might be called "quarter-section vision." Anyone who went through the thirties farming on the plains should recall that lesson. It didn't help if you were practicing good soil management on your quarter-section if all those around you were not. Their dust blew over your fences.

Early in May last year as I started to cruise around the large pools in the Bottoms, the first thing I did was startle the daylights out of four white-tailed deer. But the marsh didn't seem to impede their flight as they cut in their after-burners toward some distant trees in the northeast

MUSKRAT HOUSE IN CHEYENNE BOTTOMS

corner. A little farther along muskrat houses were abundant. Cattails are used in the construction of these houses that can be built in several hours if necessary. The houses have an opening bored in the heap of grass, from underneath, where the muskrats round out a nest. Besides this "plunge hole," the house has a couple of escape runs.

Biologists consider the muskrat a help in attempting to control the cattails. The muskrat can't do it by itself normally. In some marshes the population can expand so rapidly that what is called an "eat out" occurs, where the vegetation has all been consumed and the population crashes. The population had apparently been high earlier that summer; the biologists think that disease was the cause of the crash.

Two of the prettiest birds I came on were the American avocet and the black-necked stilt. They like shallow water to feed in, but they get away from the margin where the exposed mud meets the water. The stilt has the longest leg length in relation to body size of probably any bird; its delicate, red legs are from eight to ten inches long. The avocet is a somewhat larger bird (they are both in the avocet family, *Recurvirostridae*) and has a longer bill. Also, the avocet's bill curves upward, influencing the manner in which it gets its food. Swinging its partially opened bill from side to side under water, it stirs up food as it goes. The black-necked stilt pokes its bill straight down. Both feed on the various fly larvae, crayfish, aquatic bugs, and beetles. I believe the avocet is much more common here at the Bottoms than the stilt, but others I have talked to frequently see stilts, which winter a little farther south than the avocets; both are found in Guatemala, but the stilt is also found in northern Brazil and Peru.

The long-billed dowitcher and the dunlin were a couple of other shore birds that were numerous in May. The dunlin, which nests high in the Arctic as the long-billed dowitcher does, chooses more often, as it dashes about, to feed along the mud flats themselves. Its bill, which is slightly drooped at the end, is only between one and two inches long. Dowitchers (whose name is supposed to be from Iroquoian) sometimes move along right at the margin where the mud meets the shallow water and a little into the water, but don't seem to want to expose themselves farther out, although their bills are up to three inches long. While the dunlin winters as far south as the Texas and Louisiana coasts, the dowitcher gets as far south as Guatemala.

The stilt sandpiper feeds along the margins with the long-billed dowitcher. It has long greenish legs and a pretty rusty cheek and crown. While it has longer legs than the dowitcher, its bill is shorter. Another sandpiper, apparently common at the Bottoms though not everywhere on the plains, is Baird's sandpiper. Although it can be found feeding on the mudflats, it also is found in drier portions of the Bottoms where the grass is short. Generally the Baird's is not a prober of the mud; rather it picks what food items it can from the surface of mud or the drier, grassy ground. Both of these two sandpipers belong to a select group of long-distance migrants that fly all the way to southern Argentina.

Migration is fascinating in almost any form, but the extremes catch our attention. The little Baird's sandpiper and the stilt make it all the way down as far as southern Argentina, with some

BLACK-NECKED STILT

DUNLIN

STILT SANDPIPER

HUDSONIAN GODWIT

WHIMBREL

KILLDEER

SEMI-PALMATED PLOVER

The golden plover's path includes the Bottoms in the spring, but the plover flies down the Atlantic, in the fall return. This is an example of what is called "loop migration." The result of this is that the young plover must inherit the pathway to Argentina, and then must know to fly the overland route in the spring.

Two other plovers share very similar markings yet are quite different in their strategy. The semipalmated plover has a single dark breastband and is somewhat smaller than the killdeer, which has two dark breastbands. Their nesting habits are also similar; they merely scratch a slight depression in the gravel. The nest would seem to be extremely vulnerable, but it camouflages the eggs very effectively. I have had trouble seeing eggs when I had previously located a nest and knew the eggs were there. You won't find the semipalmated plover nesting in Kansas, however. It's another long-distance migrant and flies from the arctic all the way to Patagonia. The killdeer, on the other hand, is not only found throughout Kansas, sometimes very far from water, but is common to all four states in the Arkansas River basin.

It has been estimated that shorebird use of Cheyenne Bottoms may exceed fourteen million during the high point of the season. Record numbers of 600,000 ducks and 40,000 geese have been counted during a single census. Of the 415 species of birds in Kansas, 325 have been identified at the Bottoms. In sum, there is overwhelming evidence that Cheyenne Bottoms, like the National Grasslands, should be regarded as what it is, one of the national treasures along the Arkansas River.

———

Another small treasure of wildlife, the Maxwell Game Refuge, is to be found about fifty miles to the east of the Bottoms. It was started by a McPherson businessman within the terms of his estate during World War II. This is tall grass prairie with abundant bluestem for the herd of some two hundred buffalo to graze. Several ironies inhere in Kansas' effort to maintain a few buffalo in the state. The last buffalo was killed in Kansas in 1889, and it was declared the official state animal in 1955. Further, the starter animals that were brought from the Wichita Mountains National Wildlife Refuge in Oklahoma were the descendants of fifteen animals donated by the New York Zoological Park.

An important animal at Maxwell is the elk or wapiti. Wapiti, an Indian word for "white," refers to the elk's light-colored rump. Elk ranged over most of America until they too were nearly done in by killing. They were extirpated in Kansas in the early part of this century, and the elk at Maxwell are restocked ones. It's a stirring experience to see and hear a great bull elk bugling across the tall grass during the autumn as he attempts to gather his breeding harem.

———

ELK, MAXWELL GAME PRESERVE · 141 ·

HERD OF ELK

BULL ELK

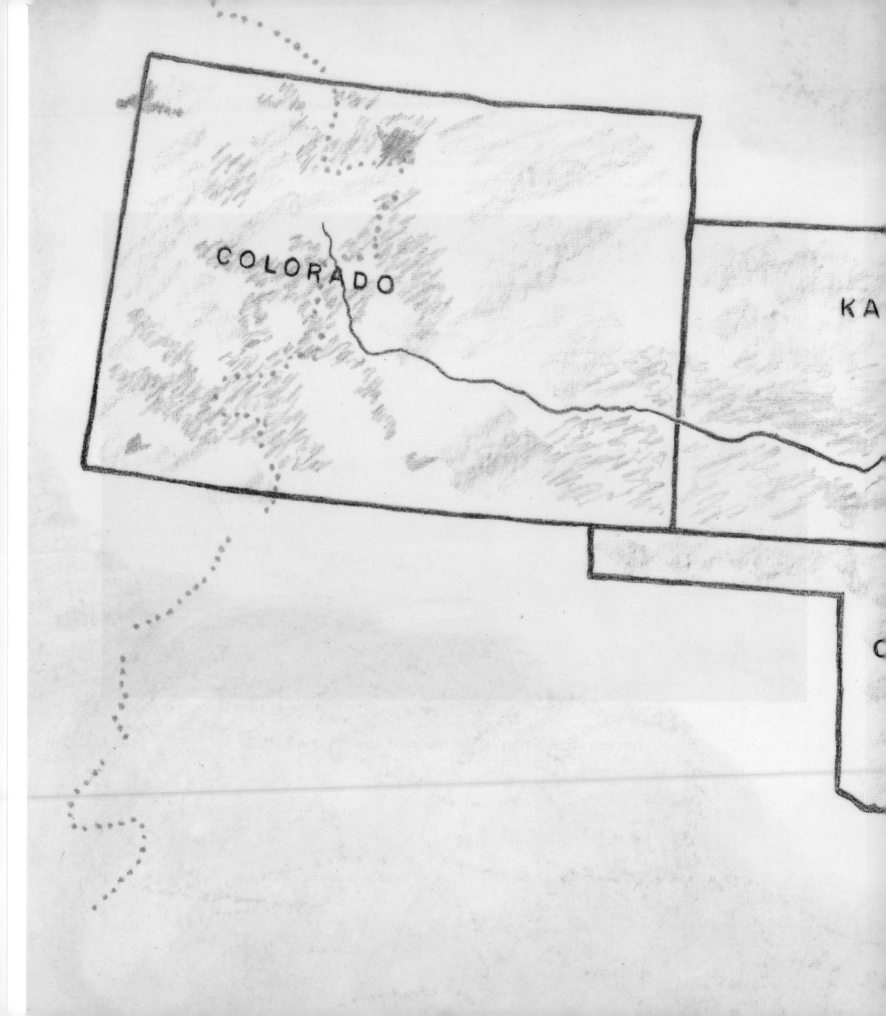

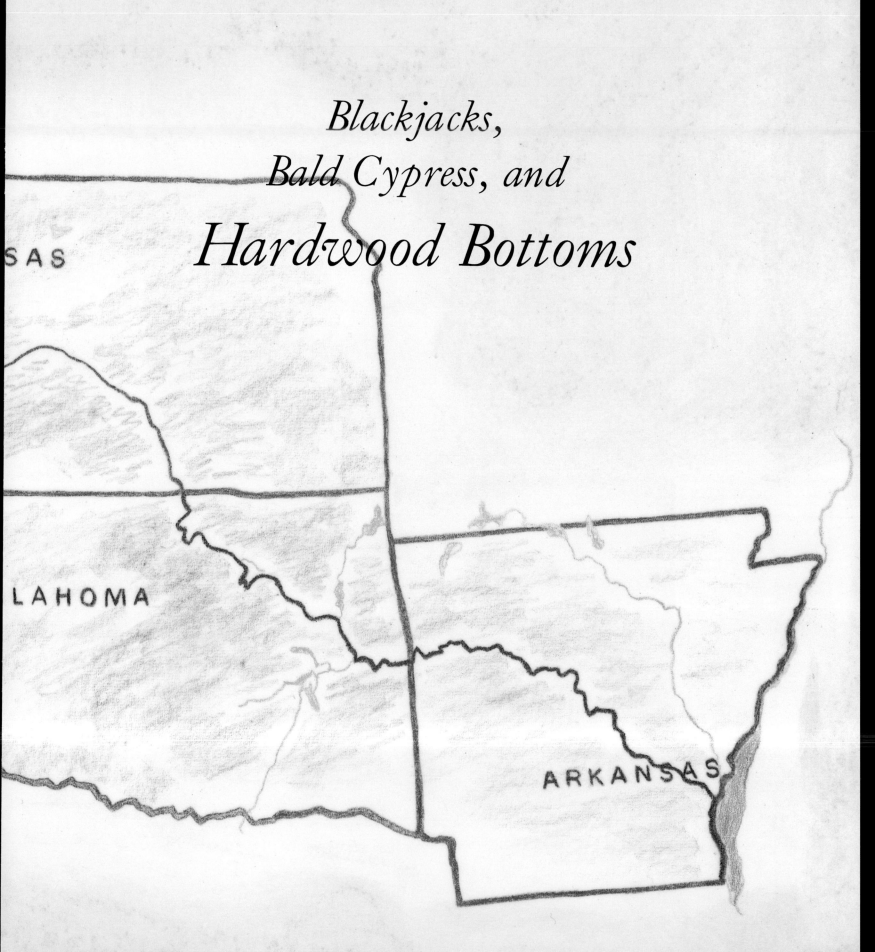

Blackjacks,
Bald Cypress, and
Hardwood Bottoms

· I52 ·   KAW DAM, PONCA CITY, OK.

THE lower Arkansas River, beginning in Oklahoma and ending in Arkansas, is resonant with names of its Indian past, beginning with the people of the Southern Sioux and ending with Southern Sioux. Soon after crossing the Kansas-Oklahoma border the river begins to build Kaw Lake (behind the dam of that name), and then sweeps westward just a little, passing by Ponca City. Both Kaw (also called Konsa, Kansas, or Ko'n-Za, meaning They-Desire-to-Run, because they split from the Osage) and Ponca are Southern Sioux. As the river leaves Kaw Dam, its east bank defines part of the boundary of Osage County, which until 1907 (when Oklahoma became a state) was the Osage Reservation, home of the largest group of Southern Sioux. Of course, these peoples had occupied much larger territories before the whites came, and only lived here after they were "removed" to what was then "Indian Territory."

The Osage area of control had, until about 1808, encompassed Kansas, Missouri, Oklahoma, and Arkansas. Gradually the Heavy Eyebrows, as the white invaders were called, reduced their territory and made treaties, broke the treaties and reduced Indian territory again, until the Osage came to rest in their final home. When they came in 1872, they settled in traditional clans, or bands, one of which is called the Big Hills people. The Big Hills people lived around the former village called Gray Horse, near the present town of Fairfax, Oklahoma, a land of bluestem prairie. The river passes through blackjack and post oak here. One June I came off the river at Salt Creek in time for an Osage dance known as I'n-Lon-Schka, or the Playground-of-the-First-Son. The Big Hills clan puts it on, but they were joined by Osage from the other clans. Later in June, or Buffalo-Pawing-Earth Moon, dances by other clans will be put on in Hominy and Pawhuska. It was after the Osage moved here in 1885 that they took up this dance from their cousins, the Poncas and Kaws. Not only do other clans come, but other tribes come: the Poncas and Kaws, of course, but the Dakota Sioux, the Sacs and Foxes, Otoes and Missouris.

This June a son of Jerry Shaw, who teaches at Wichita State, was to be privileged to "have the drum." With this privilege goes responsibility, and the boy's parents must bear the expense of the dance. There are many things special for me about I'n-Lon-Schka and about it being in Gray Horse. This is an occasion and dance not put on as a performance for outsiders like at a rodeo or pow-wow, but rather for the Osages themselves. Nowadays it may be the only time the Big Hills clan gets together and revivifies what is left of the tribal memory. Gray Horse is not even a village anymore; I believe Oklahoma classifies it as a "ghost town." There has been no "boutiquing" of the place or of the event itself. All one finds is a pavilion that is called an arbor, from the time when the dance was under the trees. In some ways it resembles an old-fashioned camp meeting with dinner on the grounds.

The dance goes on for four days. In the early afternoon of the first day, people begin putting up small wall-less tents to eat and dress under. Trunks and suitcases containing the dance costumes are placed there and soon the bright reds, blues, and yellows are hanging from lines in preparation for the first dance. There is an afternoon and an evening dance each day. The costumes run upward to a thousand dollars. Soon, one by one, the men begin to don their finery. Dazzling silken shirts, beaded belts and moccasins, and silver armbands. Especially interesting are the otter-skin tailpieces. Small bells called hawkbells are tied below the dancers' knees.

Then it is time to leave the dressing grounds. The Wah-tsde-pie'n, or town crier, announces the beginning of the procession and a double line of dancers makes its way to the arbor, someone leading a pony and two dancers bringing the drum. Down at the pavilion the singers are already seated in a circle in the center of the arena. Among the dancers are eight headmen, the Keeper-of-the-Drum, four Tail Dancers, two Whippers, and two water boys. As the drum begins and singers join in, the dancers, who are now seated around the arena, rise and begin their slow, dignified gait around the drum and singers. Suddenly the drumming will stop and everyone sits down. Only moments later the drumming begins again, this time with only the Tail Dancers dancing. They may only get started when the drums mysteriously stop again. No photographing is permitted under the pavilion while the dance is going on, in the same way that one doesn't fire off a flash during a solemn moment in church.

One bystander admitted to me that he used to dance, but that he had gotten out of shape and had to stop. It obviously takes endurance and long wind to persist through the afternoon and evening. And for four days. As the afternoon goes on, the women in the audience may join in. Some may wear traditional costume, while others don't. The occasion requires that any woman joining in must wear a blanket.

The I'n-Lon-Schka is sometimes referred to as a kind of "Give-Away Dance"; as a part of this, before the dancing ever started, blankets were handed out by the Keeper-of-the-Drum. Then there were several short speeches made about what the annual dance meant to the participants. A Christian prayer was even offered. The curious alloy of ritual dance, no doubt rooted deep in the Siouxan past, and the invocation of the Christian God, who came with the conquering Europeans, was particularly striking to me as I sat under the pavilion. I have witnessed the same passage among the Eskimos and among Guatemalan Indians. In the case of the Guatemalan Indians, they have sometimes merely taken over the Christian names to please the missionaries but are carrying out the ceremonies in their ancient way. With others, however, it is provocative how quickly the gods of the conqueror take over and put the old gods to rout. Observing the dancers dressed in the old way being watched by other Osage dressed like any contemporary Oklahoman is an image of tension. The river reflects the same tension between a time when it went its own way, the old way, and the present, with our current attempts to manage it, to dam it. The new god, "technology," is in full sway. For now. From the Kaw Dam onward, the river gods have fled. By the time the river finishes describing its part of the Osage boundary, one comes upon the huge Keystone Dam above Tulsa; by the time the Kerr-McClellan Navigation System is finished, one comes upon seventeen other locks and dams. In one sense, from the beginning of the navigation system to the mouth, there is no more river, but only "pools," as they are called. I will not try to answer the question for the Osage concerning the exchange

STATUE COMMEMORATING THE PIONEER WOMAN, PONCA CITY, OK. · 155 ·

· 156 ·   OSAGE HEADDRESS

AN OSAGE DANCER, GRAY HORSE, OK. · 157 ·

· 158 ·   YOUNG OSAGE WOMAN, GRAY HORSE, OK.

of gods. Like many others who consider such matters, though, I am uncertain about the new god of "technology" or, more precisely, Man as the new god, with technology his very powerful slave. With this slave we have poisoned the river and even dried it up in places. Rather poor gods.

John Joseph Mathews, in his book *The Osages*, writes about the I'n-Lon-Schka and describes the singers as beating the drum in a rhythm "like the heart beats of Mo'n-Sho'n, Mother Earth." What the New Man seems intent on is stopping the heartbeat, and falling upon the body of the earth in one last predatory fling. Nevermind a sustainable river, a sustainable earth, like an improvident farmer who kills his only milk cow because he wants steak tonight. All this comes to mind on a June day at Gray Horse, as the tintinnabulation of the hawkbells rings on.

———

Just above Tulsa and the Keystone Dam we meet the Cimarron once again and for the last time, for here it joins the Arkansas with its red, red waters. From the dam the river winds its way through town, and much of the time there is very little water to be seen in the wide, sandy river bed. There is no lock at Keystone, and thus there is no river navigation, even if there were enough water.

Tulsa is a very recent city, even as far as American cities go. It had formerly been in Creek territory, after they had left their land in Alabama and come to Oklahoma. There is a Creek in my family lineage, which goes back to the time of pre-removal days in Alabama. The Creek settlement that was to become Tulsa was called "Tulsey Town" in the latter nineteenth century. Then things got rolling with oil. There was a strike across the Arkansas from town at Red Fork in 1901 and another one at Glenn Pool in 1905. In 1900 the population was 1,390; in 1987 it was roughly 400,000. The city has constructed a beautiful riverside park for many blocks along the river, which is one of the most restful places in town. Wading birds grace the river and what is left of the river flow still graces the lives of those who notice it.

Although the Kerr-McClellan system was built partly to link Tulsa by water to the outside world, it is not down the Arkansas that it starts. The wide shallow river wanders on to Muskogee to join the navigation system already in progress. Actually, the Arkansas River Navigation System starts on the Verdigris River at the Port of Catoosa, east of town. The 445-mile system of locks and dams was completed in 1970 by the Corps of Engineers. From Catoosa, it's about 50 miles to the confluence of the Arkansas, the Verdigris, and the Grand (or Neosho) rivers.

It is near this confluence that Ft. Gibson was built in 1824 in preparation for the arrival and protection of the Cherokees and Choctaws. Prior to this time the area was known as Three

· 160 · KEYSTONE DAM, TULSA, OK.

TULSA FISHERMEN AT RIVERSIDE PARK · 161 ·

TULSA FROM THE RIVER

Forks. This was all Osage territory before other tribes were settled here by the U.S. government, as reflected in Thomas Nuttall's *A Journal of Travels into the Arkansas Territory During the Year 1819*. Nuttall, botanist, explorer, natural historian, and Harvard faculty member, has given us a priceless record of his travels and collecting along the Arkansas River in Arkansas and Oklahoma. He had wanted to go to the Rockies but had to turn back because of many adversities, including illness. His journal entry for July 14, 1819, remarks about the land and the vegetation where the Verdigris, Grand, and Arkansas come together.

This morning, accompanied by Mr. Prior, I walked over a portion of the alluvial land of the Verdigris, the fertility of which was sufficiently obvious in the disagreeable and smothering luxuriance of the tall weeds, with which it was overrun. This neck of land, situated betwixt Grand river and the Verdigris, is about two miles wide, free from inundation, and covered with larger trees than any other I had seen since leaving Fort Smith. Among them were lofty scarlet oaks, ash, hackberry, and whole acres of nettles. . . .

On the same day, but earlier in the *Journal*, he observed the "slaty sand-stone" as he approached Three Forks. From this point on the Arkansas on to Little Rock, nearly all that the river traveler sees is sedimentary rock from that ancient inland sea that we found rising and falling evidence of on the plains. Generally it is layers of shale and sandstone, with some occasional limestone.

Cruising down the river from Three Forks is a pleasant experience nowadays, first because you can move with the river, unlike Nuttall's initial upstream odysssey. And a motor makes it easier, if noisier. One begins in Cherokee country. As a matter of fact, the Cherokee, along with the Chickasaw and Choctaw, own a ninety-six-mile stretch of the river bed ending just west of Ft. Smith.

There are lots of reasons to stop in Muskogee, but two good ones that come readily to mind are Slick's Bar-B-Que and the art of Jerome Tiger. Slick's place is laid back, unassuming. You might miss it if you hadn't been told exactly where it was. But his barbecue has been written up in national food magazines, even drawing celebrities like Jimmy Connors, who is reputed to have said he liked Slick's barbecue because it made him jump higher over the net when he won a match. In any case, it's a place known to aficionados of the barbecue underground, and, further, a place where roughnecks and millionaire oil men all sit down together.

Jerome Tiger, whose art can be seen at the Tiger Gallery and also at the Five Civilized Tribes Museum in Muskogee, was a full-blood Creek-Seminole, a high school dropout, a street and ring fighter who died at the age of twenty-six of a gunshot wound. Self-trained, he was one hell of an artist. Even if you can't afford to buy any of the originals, you can marvel at the poignant "Last Journey," the bitter-sweet figures dancing around a fire at the "Stomp Dance," and feel the prophetic optimism of "War to Peace, Death to Life."

Downriver several more miles you lock through Webbers Falls Lock and Dam, but the landmark of the modest falls is gone, along with numerous other landmarks referred to in

THE FAMOUS "SLICK" OF SLICK'S BAR-B-QUE, MUSKOGEE, OK.

Nuttall's *Journal*. He noted that the cascade was two or three feet high and that their boat went aground for several hours there. "It appears," he wrote, "to form one of the first obstacles of consequence in the navigation of the Arkansa."

Not long after leaving the Webbers Falls Lock, the Illinois River empties its waters into the Arkansas. Nuttall notes that the water coming in from the north is clear, while the river water from the south (and west) is red and muddy. The substantial tributary, the Canadian, enters soon, just above the Sequoyah Wildlife Refuge. Its mouth is largely obscured by the sweeping shallows and numerous rock jetties. Naturally, the channel of the Arkansas is thrust to the opposite bank. One is now in the large Robert Kerr Reservoir where all the open water is much different from Nuttall's time. Like any large, shallow body of water, it can become rapidly dangerous for small cruisers like my own and I am always glad to get on across and lock through.

On one trip I was cruising with Mike Nichols, the technical director of the Arkansas Repertory Theater in Little Rock. We came at evening time to one of my favorite places in Leflore County, a place by the name of Deadman's Slough. Beyond the sandbar where we pitched our tents and beyond some rock revetments was a wide area of shallows drawing all sorts of birds. As always, the delicate snowy egret arrested my attention and somehow arrested the evening, or at least brought it to focus. Until the sun went down, the snowy kept up his fishing. Sometimes he moved one yellow foot (on a black leg) along the silty-sandy bottom, stirring up food and then the sure, black beak would thrust home, retrieving perhaps a small crayfish. Occasionally he would run skittering across the dark shallows, after creatures I could not see from our distant campsite; sometimes he was successful, sometimes not.

The other compelling reason for stopping here for the evening was to be near the Spiro Mounds. For any Arkansas River buff, the mounds loom in importance, right on the river bank. Now, of course, there is not as much to see in the well-tended park maintained by the state of Oklahoma as there was eight hundred years ago, unless one can fill in some of the missing pieces of the site from archaeological publications, or remember his walks through the little museum on the grounds. Yet this was one of the great ceremonial complexes in southeastern America. It is still a very mysterious place, and much of its past will always be closed off to us and to archaeologists as well. Presently, the state of affairs in archaeology is such that the specialist cannot agree what descriptive or categorical terms to use for it. The themes and objects have been called part of a "Southern Cult," and also a "Southeastern Ceremonial Complex." No one means anymore, if they ever did, that it was part of a "cult" in the sociological sense. But, as James Griffin has remarked, "It contained one of the most concentrated deposits of ceremonial material ever uncovered in the United States." Another writer has called this site the King Tutankhamen's tomb of the eastern United States.

The site was probably first occupied between A.D. 700 and 950 and perhaps reached a peak of importance, economically and culturally, between A.D. 1200 and 1350. The sad part of the story of Spiro has made the entire story very unclear for us. Between 1933 and 1935, "commercial excavators" leased the site from the owner and largely gutted the place. The authenticity

of some of the objects will forever be held in question. Yet the story that can be pieced together, along with the stories of ceremonial complexes that existed at the same time in other parts of the Southeast, is an exciting one.

Americans had changed quite a bit since the time of the people up on Big Sandy at the Olsen-Chubbock site in Colorado. Now, along with their hunting and gathering, they were farming, too, that necessary prerequisite to staying in one place and generally having the time to generate the beautiful objects that were found in the burials of the tallest mound, now called Craig Mound. Besides the seeds gathered, the people were cultivating squash, maize, and eventually beans.

Burials were now taking on much more importance in the lives of the people. At least the burials of important people. Characteristic of many such mounds across the eastern United States, these became larger with time, for here there were nine successive phases of use. Craig Mound, in particular, was in continued use as a mortuary and a place of deposition for the burials. This was the great mortuary that produced so much of the rich materials now in private collections and museums about the country. Here were found human and animal effigy pipes of clay and stone (such as the famous "Big Boy" pipe now kept at the University of Arkansas at Fayetteville), monolithic stone axes, embossed copper plates, effigies of cedar, and engraved shell objects, to name just a few of the important artifacts. One of the conch shells is engraved with a water spider that likely reflects the gift of fire. The story goes that the spider walks on the surface of a lake to a burning tree, and brings fire to the people on its back.

What is particularly important about the objects is that they reflect the very wide and extensive network of exchange. Thus, seven or eight hundred years ago, objects and perhaps food stuffs were being exchanged from Mississippi to Minnesota, and from Oklahoma to the Atlantic coast. Shell gorgets that were made in northern Georgia or eastern Tennessee, perhaps, have been found at Spiro. In a limited sort of way, Spiro was the Tulsa or Little Rock of its day.

Upland and to the west of the burial mounds near Craig Mound are six other mounds surrounding an oval plaza. The largest structure is a truncated pyramid that covers more area than Craig. Likely this group of six structures was used for ceremonial occasions. Generally, Spiro was not used as a "village" or principal place of habitation, but more as we use our churches—for special occasions. The complexity of mound building (remember that the dirt was probably carried up the mound in baskets) indicates a more structured social organization than might be necessary for hunter-gatherers. Further, it is hypothesized that leaders were hereditary chieftains of a special kinship group. Such hereditary lineage would serve to reinforce structure and give continuity to the group. The death of such a chieftain would be an important and far-reaching event.

There is a provocative richness to the ritual objects and religious symbols found in sites of the Southern Cult. There are Greek-styled crosses, swastikas, hands with eyes in the palms, bi-lobed "arrows" or warclub heads, and plumed or feathered serpents. Each site had its own

THE BIG BOY PIPE, SPIRO MOUNDS

SHELL GORGET, SPIRO MOUNDS

particular artistic style, even though the symbols might be held in common. The Spiro site is clearly marked by the Caddoan culture, which reflects, at some point in its development, the influence of Middle America. It has been suggested that some of this influence may have come by way of Aztec traders, traveling along the same old ways that the later traveler, Spaniard Cabeza de Vaca, used. Such common ceramic themes as the plumed serpent and the stylized swastika designs support this, and the presence of objects depicting the "long-nosed god" seem to come from Mexico. One very striking ceramic object nearly ten inches tall is called "Human Sacrifice Effigy Clay Pipe." The victim is much smaller than the executioner (perhaps this is a child), and a blade-shaped weapon is buried halfway in the victim's head. Such a scene demonstrates, no doubt, the practice of retainer sacrifice for the burial of important figures. This, too, may derive from Middle America.

As the last snowy egret leaves Deadman's Slough and heads for the place where he will feel safe in the dark until the return of the sun, it is appropriate to speculate just what engine drove the Spiro people, what idea urged them to take special care of their dead chieftain and drove them to be sometimes willing retainers in the journey he was about to take. For now the individual is much more subordinated to the group, to communal life, and it is through this more structured, complex group that he must face not only life, one side of the world's face, but death, the other side.

Looking at the intricate designs of a shell gorget or a sheet of copper from Spiro lets you know in a powerfully instructive way how different the vision of these people was from the vision of those who may have etched a bison or an elk on a rock shelter wall. While talking about the hunters of Europe, Joseph Campbell contrasts their art with the new planting societies and observes that "we do not find, even in this latest stage of the hunting period, anything that could be termed a geometrical organization, anything suggesting the concept of a definitely circumscribed field in which a number of disparate elements have been united or fused into one aesthetic whole by a rhythm of beauty." He goes on to remark on the sudden appearance of organized circular compositions of geometrical and abstract motifs on the pottery of planting societies in the Tigris-Euphrates area, sometimes with the swastika, sometimes with a bird or a double-headed ax. Surely Spiro and other such sites reflect much the same development.

The people of Spiro may have been people in transition between making sense of the world as hunters, compelled to propitiate the spirits of the animals they were killing, and making sense of the world as planters, compelled to propitiate the spirits of the plant world. This world was much more obviously bound to the yearly cycle of planting and harvesting, and a cycle obviously bound to the stars and planets. What seems equally clear is that the artistic and religious efforts of the people at Spiro cannot be explained purely in economic terms. The human sacrifices and the decorated objects placed in the grave with the chieftain sprang from some deeper need to hold the people's world intact, and to perpetuate it. Their art evinces the circumscribed field that parallels, in a suggestive way, the circumscribed fields of their planting, of

PLOWING THE OLD WAY IN EASTERN OKLAHOMA

their ceremonial grounds, and even of their lives. Adopting the constraints of form, their art and their religious impulses release a striking inflorescence hundreds of years before Europeans had ever heard of them. They realized all of it beside this quiet river where Mike and I now sit looking more carefully at the stars than we ever do, or can, in the brightly lit city, but now not cut off from the mysteries of this unfathomable universe.

From Deadman's Slough we locked through and cruised the few miles to Ft. Smith. On the north side of the river, still in Oklahoma, we passed Moffett Bottoms, which is a favorite with Audubon Club members as well as bird and animal watchers in general. It lies just above the confluence of the Poteau River, which is right on the Oklahoma-Arkansas border. It was at this confluence, then known as Belle Point, that Major Stephen Long chose the site for the fort and named it after his commanding general, Thomas A. Smith. The purpose of the fort was to end hostilities among the Indians, namely those of the Osage against the Cherokee, Quapaw, and Comanche. The fort was under the command of Major William Bradford when Nuttall arrived in April of 1819. At first Nuttall thought Bradford would not allow him to continue his river journey, because he was entering Indian Territory, but the difficulties were fortunately worked out. Nuttall had numerous troubles with the Osage before he was through. The pipe of peace was not smoked among the tribes until five months after Nuttall passed through.

Obviously Ft. Smith has grown considerably since those days, and its growth, concurrent with growth up and down this part of the Arkansas River, presents a problem. That problem is lack of water. Health departments will not allow use of the Arkansas River as a potential water supply because of the ever-present danger of an oil spill or the like. Tom Foti, the field ecologist for the Arkansas Natural Heritage Commission, sums it up in his monograph *The Natural Divisions of Arkansas.*

There are not really very good water supplies in the Arkansas River Valley and when growth and development take place, people must look for new and enlarged water supplies. When they do, they very often look to the streams that flow out of the Ozark mountains to the north. However, these streams are valuable scenic and recreational resources themselves. Consequently, the people of the Arkansas River Valley are going to be faced with some very difficult trade-offs between preserving these streams as a scenic and recreational resource or developing them as water supply reservoirs.

Lee Creek, one of the finest streams I've ever canoed, empties into the Arkansas at Ft. Smith. It was mentioned in Nuttall's *Journal,* and his identification stuck instead of the French name, Perpillon. More than a year ago, friends told me that there was a plan afoot by Ft. Smith city

tail up and down, calling "peet-weet" as he hunted in his solitary way. Coots croaked ahead and made frantic efforts to get away, only to settle a little farther downstream. Twice we had the treat of seeing blue-winged teal hens become flustered trying to hide their recently hatched broods and, in the attempt to draw us away, leave the babies behind. A magical event occurred each time the hen said something in blue-winged teal and the babies would disappear; even though we might move closer for a better look, there was never a sign. They apparently froze in place under some bank overhang or bush.

Along the way other flashes in the world of natural being surprised us. The rarer least bittern of the dark phase clung to a bush in the water and was content to let us come close, let us be if we would let it be. Farther along, the broad-winged hawk wheeled overhead, and soon the ubiquitous red-tailed hawk joined us. If any bird is representative of the whole river, it is the red-tailed hawk. I was quite used to him in the lower river, and was especially gratified to see this old acquaintance in regular intervals all the way through Kansas and Colorado. How I was stirred by seeing a red-tail emerge from a roadside ditch with a writhing snake still in its talons, the outcome of which fracas I was not to know.

The people of Crawford County in Arkansas and those of Sequoyah in Oklahoma (Ft. Smith is in Sebastian County where the water will go) need to come and see the rock faces of the high bluffs on Lee Creek, rock faces that are every bit as beautiful and awe-inspiring as those of the much-touted Buffalo River to the north, a National Wilderness river. It's an old song, but it must be sung again: just as Colorado is realizing, the "growth" that has resulted from people moving in because of the natural heritage is going to be the knife that kills the goose that laid the golden egg. Growing larger physically is only useful for a child. For a mature adult, growth means something else.

Before our time on Lee Creek was over, we had seen three different swallowtails and some sulfurs, the great and little blue herons, several woodpeckers, cardinals, and eastern pewees. And as if Lee Creek itself didn't want my brother Tom to go away without an epiphany of national symbolic importance, he saw his first bald eagle, winging across the white water and the limestone cliffs, coming to rest on a tree branch, the better to surveil its domain. Like any other epiphany worth its name, this was a pointer, directing our attention, urging us to be vigilant as we surveil our common wilderness.

As the river leaves Ft. Smith it sweeps south, then straightens out east again and brushes the army's big area occupied by Ft. Chaffee. Another sweeping turn north, then eastward, and finally through the wine country of central Arkansas: vineyards with names like Wiederkehr and Post. From the top of a high ridge you can see that some of these Swiss settlers had picked out valleys that reminded them of home, and of course growing grapes. As the river bottoms

DOGWOOD

SHOOTING STAR

DESERTED FARM HOUSE NEAR SUBIACO, AR.

BENEDICTINE ABBEY AT SUBIACO, AR.

out with another south and eastward swing, it is just north of Paris. Paris, Arkansas. Down the road is another thread in the river's skein—the Benedictine abbey at Subiaco, a little town named after the one in Italy where Benedict started out in a cave in the fifth century. Like its counterpart in Cañon City, Colorado, the largest part of its land is devoted to agriculture. The interesting architecture of these Benedictine monasteries justifies singling them out for notice in the river valley. More importantly, these communities come to mind as examples of using the land along the river in a thoughtful way, not attempting to put nature to the test in some inquisitorial fashion, or to subdue it, but rather serving as stewards of the land which, in turn, helps support them in what is, perhaps, man's principal preoccupation of discovering why he finds himself born within this natural world and what is its ultimate ground.

South of Paris is Magazine Mountain, the highest point in the state at 2,753 feet. Reputedly, French hunters gave it this homely name, which means storehouse or warehouse. It deserves a more interesting name, because Magazine Mountain is a special place along the Arkansas River. A site of great diversity, it contains numerous rare plants, insects and animals.

The geological formation of Magazine is similar to that of other such flat-top, or mesa-like, mountains on this side of the river, including Petit Jean and Mt. Nebo. It is made up of Pennsylvanian-age sedimentary rock, with largely alternating strata of sandstone and shale. For example, the top is sandstone about eight hundred feet thick, then shale for seven hundred feet. Magazine is a synclinal mountain, which means that the rock strata bend downward toward the middle. Thus, as you drive up the mountain, you notice that the strata (generally visible only in the clear strata of sedimentary rock) tilt inward toward the mountain. In such a synclinal fold, the youngest rocks are inside the fold. The syncline was squeezed upward at some point, and then eroded, but the sandstone that now caps the mountain was the most resistant stone. There is some speculation that Magazine was an ancient connector between the Ozarks and the Ouachitas. A part of such speculation is the hypothesis that at one time the Arkansas River did not flow through as it now does from Oklahoma to the Mississippi. Perhaps there was a river flowing westward from here, and another ancient river flowing eastward to the Mississippi. The faster flowing headwaters of the eastern river eroded backward, and ultimately the two became the one river we have now.

The French naming of Magazine may have turned out to be prophetic, for it has indeed turned out to be a storehouse of plants and animals of great diversity. They might not be here if Magazine could have been plowed under or totally logged. It is now in the Ozark National Forest and is presently under what is called "administrative protection." If this protection were lifted, the mountain might be in trouble. At the present time, however, the U.S. Forest Service is working with local agencies like the Arkansas Natural Heritage Commission to hold the line.

There are three primary vegetative communities at Magazine: upland deciduous forest, evergreen forest, and glade-type grassland. The upland deciduous forest is generally on the north-facing slope and north rim of the mountain. One big reason for this is that this side

SEDIMENTARY STRATA NEAR DARDANELLE, AR.

retains more moisture than the southern-facing slope. From the twenty-four inches of rain in Leadville to the fourteen inches in the shortgrass prairie, we have now come to fifty or fifty-five inches at Magazine, and there is a much longer growing season than the alpine tundra. Instead of some sixty days of growing time, there may be two hundred forty. On the north rim and slopes there are massive red oaks, white oaks, and several hickories, with smaller numbers of black gum and maple. At the top, where the soil is poorer, we find post oak and blackjack in abundance.

The oak-hickory forest of the north slope may be the most mature stand in the Arkansas River valley. Some of the red oaks are three feet in diameter. Appropriately, another oak in the "red oak group" is the Nuttall oak found on Magazine. This helps us to remember Nuttall looking up this way 168 years ago. At the present time, the Forest Service does not permit any logging or new roads, for which they should be soundly commended.

A number of plant and animal species on Magazine are found nowhere else. On the north slope near Brown's Springs and Cameron Bluff we have the maple-leaved oak. Until someone discovers it elsewhere, the result of its entire evolutionary heritage is found only at Magazine. Below the cliffs on the talus slope is the Magazine Mountain middle-toothed land snail, also found only here. Tom Allen, an entomologist at Fayetteville, Arkansas, believes that he will ultimately find twenty-five insect species here that are completely new to science. Altogether on Magazine there are at least 531 plant species. Of these, fifteen are considered either very rare or of special interest because of their limited or disjunct distribution. On the north slope, these include the hay-scented fern, Rocky Mountain woodsia and a pipewort (*Eriocaulon kornickianum*). The woodsia on Magazine is found in only three centers of dispersal, the other two being in the Appalachians and the Rockies; and this disjunct distribution is extremely interesting to the botanist. Such a plant can lead to many useful inferences about our botanical and our geological past.

The south-facing slope reflects the fact that it gets less moisture. Marvelous gnarled red cedars are at the rim, not far from Signal Hill, the actual spot that is the highest point in the state. On at least one occasion on Signal Hill, the Stewardship Chief of the Arkansas Natural Heritage Commission, Bill Pell, and I came upon a considerable array of fatigue-clad soldiers practicing their artillery coordinates as they peered through binoculars out over Petit Jean River, a tributary of the Arkansas. On a clear day from Cameron Bluff on the north rim, you might be able to look to the northwest and see Cherokee Prairie, the largest totally protected virgin prairie in Arkansas.

Besides the red cedar, there is short-leaf pine below, and those stalwart adapters to poor soil and little rain, the blackjack and the post oak. Just upslope from some of the gnarled cedars on Signal Hill is the interesting and rare herb, *Paronychia virginica*.

Generally there are few sharp lines between vegetative communities, but rather a slope of change, with transition zones where different plants will take over. This is true of the terrain

FUNGUS ON THE FOREST FLOOR, MAGAZINE MOUNTAIN

REINDEER LICHEN, MAGAZINE MOUNTAIN

MAPLE LEAF OAK, MAGAZINE MOUNTAIN

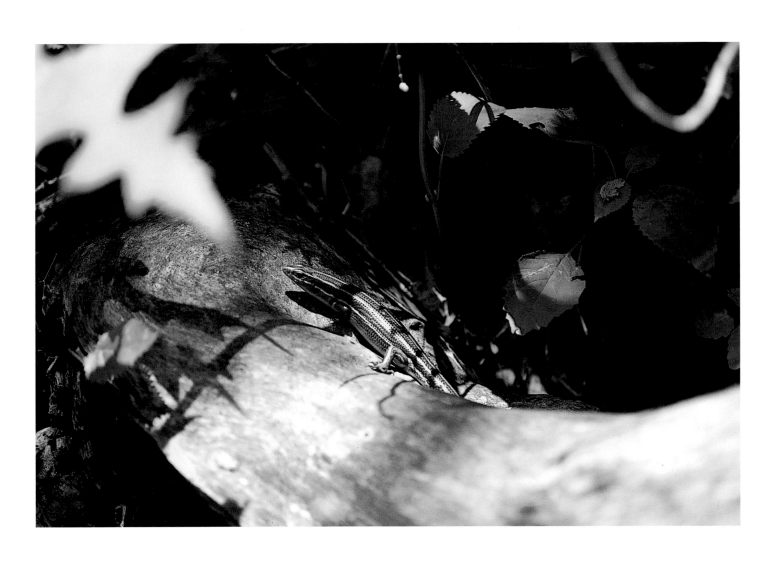

FIVE-LINE SKINK, MAGAZINE MOUNTAIN

· 192 ·   PARONYCHIA, MAGAZINE MOUNTAIN

INDIAN PAINTBRUSH, CHEROKEE PRAIRIE, AR.   · 193 ·

· 194 ·   WHITE WILD INDIGO

CARDINAL FLOWERS WITH BUTTERFLIES · 195 ·

between the evergreen community and the red cedar glade-type grasslands. The rufous-crowned sparrow finds this location just right for nesting, and this is the only known nesting place for this bird in Arkansas.

There is a great deal we do not know about the relationships between the various elements in a community (including the human elements). In the presence of the rufous-crowned sparrow, we can only feel instructed in self-restraint as we go along striking down diverse forests to plant a single species, plowing the prairie to seed it all in a monoculture of wheat, or chopping a running river into pools. Unless some people had kept their eyes upon the place of the sparrow, another wrong kind of silence would have come to pass.

The prairie openings in the glades have likely been maintained in the past by fires either caused by lightning or set accidentally or on purpose by Indians. Unless many prairies are burned in some way, the shrubs and eventually the trees can take over. With bad luck, the wind can come up suddenly, or change directions, and a good idea can turn into sheer horror.

With the advent of farming throughout the Great Plains and also in Arkansas, huge burns from lightning or human accident diminished. Now we have to imitate nature. One evening I was with Bill Pell and Ken Smith over at Cherokee in part to check on how the prairie had come back from its last burn and in part to validate the presence of the prairie-mole cricket. Like the ornate box turtle, which we also found, the prairie-mole cricket is evidence of true prairie in good condition. Ken showed me a life-sized picture of one and I thought I might have some trouble, because the latest word on how to catch this cricket is to plunge your hand down behind his burrow entrance and cut off his escape. But this wasn't any cricket I had ever put on a bream hook. He looked like he might be able to fight back. Only the male would be chirping. He had a deep tunnel to escape in, but just below the surface of the ground he had hollowed out a chamber that served to amplify his call. Ken played a tape of what one sounded like, and then we split up. I felt like I was being initiated into the insect version of a snipe hunt. Every chirp of a bird or small critter sounded like a possibility, but I wasn't sure I would recognize one, anyway. I got back up with Bill and we went off to another area. He wasn't sure he knew one positively, either. Maybe it made a very faint sound. Ken might have had the volume up on his tape recorder. I knew I was going to have a hard time explaining to a local sheriff's deputy what I was doing out here.

Then they started. Every female cricket within half a mile would have known she was being courted. Most of the time the sounds would stop as we drew near; perhaps the males could feel the slight vibrations of our steps. Finally Bill knew he had one, and plunged his hand behind the voice chamber to cut off escape . . . and nearly broke his hand because this soil was not the plunging kind. No cricket. Fortunately for the Nature Conservancy records and the Commission's, Ken came back victorious. We should all feel fortunate that prairie-mole crickets don't get larger than they do.

A HOLLY IN WINTER · 197 ·

Eastward the river widens considerably into what is known as Lake Dardanelle. It is highly visible from Interstate Highway 40 to the north, and the lake sits jewel-like in its bowl of rock. What is also highly visible as one draws near Russellville is the looming cooling tower of a nuclear plant. In a quite literal way, and then in a symbolic way, the presence of the reactors is portentous.

The litany of difficulties involved with nuclear power generation has been produced for some of us so often that we are numbed against hearing it again. For others, the problems are obvious only in the wake of some spectacular disaster of human error that makes the national television news, disasters such as those at Three Mile Island or Chernobyl. The difficulties are always there, and as silent as the reactors of Arkansas Power and Light Nos. 1 and 2. In a literal sense, we have not solved, and may never be able to solve, the problem of disposing of the radioactive waste currently being produced along with the electricity and the ultimate effects of that waste upon all the earth's water. At least the United States and Great Britain have stopped dumping it into the sea in concrete containers. But where? When the salt domes came up for a test, up river in Lyons, Kansas, the Atomic Energy Commission felt it had a permanent solution. But the Kansas Geologic Survey and the Kansas Geological Society said the site should be abandoned. William W. Hambleton, then director of the Kansas Geologic Survey, wrote, "There is nothing more important than recognizing a dead horse early and burying it with as little ceremony as possible." He was referring to the site itself, but the "dead horse" of radioactive waste still needs to be buried. No matter where it is put, the death-dealing potential persists from a few years to many generations. It is important to emphasize that the dangers inherent in radioactive waste result when everything is working perfectly in a nuclear plant.

There is the other, darker side of nuclear power generation, an example of which we witnessed in April of 1986 at Chernobyl, where the plant exploded. The direct results included a thousand immediate injuries, at least thirty-one deaths, 135,000 people evacuated and a material loss of over three billion dollars. Which point brings us to the symbolic meaning one may draw from the reactor near Russellville, or any other, anywhere. Part of that meaning is made clear in an observation by Albert Einstein in 1946. "Our world faces a crisis as yet unperceived by those possessing the power to make great decisions for good or evil. The unleashed power of the atom has changed everything save our modes of thinking, and thus we drift toward unparalleled catastrophe." No one needs to be convinced about the awesome power of the unleashed atom; the power of the atom leashed, in these reactors looming on the river, is just as profound.

The urgency for changing our ways of thinking is dramatized by nuclear reactors, but is also visible in less powerful technologies. As I observed earlier about the effect of the horse on the Plains Indian, a new "technology," and the effect of the gun and tractor on the Indian and the European settler, certain ways of thinking that had served very well for millennia may suddenly become destructive. Even the same bad habits were not as destructive earlier. A bunch of drunks on horses are not nearly as likely to kill themselves or others as they are in cars. The horses might even take them home at night.

ATOMIC REACTORS NEAR RUSSELLVILLE, AR.

MEADOWBROOK, NEAR FOX, AR.

Every change in technology is not the same as every other, even when they seem to be of equal degree. This has its analogy in the rising temperature of water. From 30 degrees to 31 degrees is not the same as from 32 degrees to 33 degrees, or similarly 211 degrees and 212 degrees. What you have is a dramatic change in the state of being. This has its instructive counterpart in pre-industrial and post-industrial societies, pre-nuclear and post-nuclear. Changes in the state of being have resulted. Whereas there was once a common understanding that man was only a part of nature and did not dominate it, there has now been a shift to at least the illusion that we are in charge of nature. For the briefest of times, we can indeed seem to dominate it, we can seem to be gods. The illusion will be dispelled when we have made the planet as radioactive as the sun.

The likelihood of more accidents similar to Chernobyl has little to do with whether or not mankind is becoming more evil. It has partly to do with an unexamined aggressiveness in the attitude of the technologists: the natural world is looked at merely as a resource to be mined, dammed, or exploded. Concurrent with this is the change in the kind and complexity of power now available. North of the river in Fox, Arkansas, is the Meadowcreek Project, which is in part focused on research in applied ecology and renewable energy systems. David Orr, one of the principals at Meadowcreek, has written the following:

The reasons [that there likely will be a serious accident similar to Three Mile Island] are to be found in the awesome complexity of nuclear engineering where interactions between component systems are difficult to understand at best. Other problems, including core embrittlement, are proving to be equally awesome, both financially and technically. The result is a technology vulnerable to small and often trivial events. Nuclear safety depends on heroic performance in design and construction, and equally heroic performance thereafter in maintenance, operation and security. We believe assumptions of heroic performance are unrealistic for tightly coupled systems with catastrophic potential.

Surely no one doubts that we have the capacity to make a machine that we do not have the reflexes to run. If all we could do with a car, for instance, was start it, if we had no way of stopping it, we would be fools to get in it. Why would anyone make a car that he couldn't handle? Because, some technologists argue, if something *can* be done, it *ought* to be done. Yet merely because someone can jump from an airplane with no parachute is no recommendation for doing so. We also hear that if we don't go ahead and jump, someone else will. Better that we spent our time talking him out of it.

Whether it concerns uranium ore polluting the ground water in Colorado, or unrestricted center-pivot irrigation in Kansas, or nuclear reactors and their radioactive waste in Arkansas, this river is here to instruct us in restraint.

· 202 ·   OLD IRON BRIDGE, MORRILTON, AR.

After passing Russellville and the town of Dardanelle across the bridge (which incidentally has one of the great catfish restaurants right on the river, the Catfish Inn), the Arkansas turns southerly and is soon out of sight from the road. Often now along the sandbars you see lots of Canada geese that are part of the resident population. These birds originated in the Holla Bend National Wildlife Refuge that borders the southern bank of the river. Besides Canadas, there are huge flocks of snow geese. During the fall and winter months, bald eagles have followed the migrating water fowl. Bald eagles nested regularly in Arkansas until the mid-1950s but then became an endangered species through loss of habitat and the use of farm pesticides. Thus, those once seen along the Arkansas now have nested elsewhere. In the 1980s a handful nested here, but only one, in the White River National Wildlife Refuge, produced any young. Between 1980 and 1982, at least twenty-nine bald eagles were killed or wounded by illegal shooting in Arkansas.

After walking the sandbars near Holla Bend, Mike Nichols and I resumed our cruise. Towards evening we pulled into the shallows beneath the shadow of Petit Jean Mountain. With the water only inches deep in some places the great blue herons were having what looked like a lot of luck fishing. A yellow-crowned night heron stroked its way across the evening sky with an occasional "quark" for good measure. Before the light died away, we hustled about looking for driftwood for our evening fire. Mike was soon following some large bobcat tracks across the unblemished sand. They ended in a small flurry, marked by several feathers.

High above, the grave of petit Jean kept watch on the summer sky. The romantic story goes that a young Frenchwoman followed her fiance to this country. She came over disguised as a cabin boy and was known as "petit Jean," little John. When the group stopped at this mountain, she fell ill and died. Only then was the cabin boy discovered to be a young woman.

There are numerous rock shelters in the valley that contain rock art, and the best known to the public is Rockhouse Cave on Petit Jean. It's a large shelter, with the faint remains of pictographs on the walls and ceiling, their red lines sketching deer, a paddlefish, and various geometric motifs. As with any public site that is not under heavy guard, the public has vandalized these walls with spray paint. Test excavations made in this shelter have produced projectile points of the Early and Middle Archaic periods (from 6000 B.C.). Later levels in the shelter have revealed potsherds and points from the Late Prehistoric (from A.D. 700). Like all rock art, these pictographs are very difficult to date.

During the night, small fish broke the water near our tents, scurrying to avoid their pursuers. The moon was almost full and there seemed to be considerable feeding going on. To our surprise next morning, the boat was aground. After we had struggled for an hour, two bass fishermen came along and gave us a hand. Sometimes the dams that have generating stations suddenly cause the river level to drop. The fishermen complained that this had affected the fishing a good bit. One of them said he had gone aground only a few weeks before. On a previous morning, I had discovered the boat much further out in the river, the anchor being dragged along by the newly released water.

CANADA GEESE

DAWN AT PETIT JEAN

PICTOGRAPH AT PETIT JEAN

VANDALISM, PETIT JEAN

LEAST TERNS

Later that morning, a few miles above Toad Suck Dam, Mike and I came to a series of sandbars that are least tern nesting grounds. The inland least tern is endangered in both Kansas and Arkansas. This tern was nearly eliminated on the continent by professional hunters who were killing them to secure their feathers for women's hats. They came under "full" protection in 1913. Full protection then meant no shooting, but since we are now killing them in new ways through habitat destruction, the meaning of full protection has had to be broadened. Inland, they nest on sandbars in big rivers. They merely make a small, unlined scrape and lay their one or two eggs. They are completely vulnerable on the sand to human activities. Nesting sites have been destroyed by three-wheelers and dune buggies racing back and forth on the bars. I have seen people gathering tern eggs and couldn't help wondering what they expected to do with them. Of course, there are also natural predators such as turtles and blue herons. But terns have shown their ability to flourish among only natural predators.

Along the Arkansas their habitat is under siege in two additional ways. If there is a flood, or a sudden release of water at the dams, their nests are simply washed away. In 1969, an entire nesting site disappeared when Lock and Dam 13 was closed for a time. In the second place, channelization projects can eliminate or flood the sites.

As the name least tern suggests, it is our smallest tern, with a wing span of about twenty inches. They bring considerable pleasure as one watches them dive for minnows or other small fish. If it is courtship time, the male will bring a sample for his potential mate to show that he is a good provider. And good he must be, for when the eggs hatch he will have to make steady roundtrips. Should you get close to a scrape during the nesting season, you are the target of numerous swooping dives and you think surely you will be struck by their bills. That, however, is not the only worry; as they pull out of their dives, they may evacuate their bowels with a terrible precision.

I stopped in to have a chat with the lockmaster at Toad Suck. On this day the water was running between 14,000 and 19,000 cubic feet per second, which was just ambling along. Small craft warnings go out when the flow hits 70,000 cfs. The lockmaster said that people don't heed the warnings sometimes, not realizing how swiftly the sand bars or bottoms can change. One day they may be swimming from a sand bar and the next morning step off into a hole and be swept away.

Naturally people in nearby Conway are proud of their dam's name. Nobody can hear it without doing a double-take. The story is that when there was only a ferry here, before there was a bridge, there was a tavern on one side where the boatmen would stop in. One observer remarked that the boatmen's faces were so swollen from sucking up their beer, they resembled toads. At least, that is one version of the story. People from Conway have an annual festival called "Toad Suck Daze."

The lock at Toad Suck, similar to the others on the river, is six hundred feet long and one hundred ten feet wide, which accommodates three barges across. At this particular lock the lift

SOLOMON'S SEAL

BUTTERFLY WEED

PINNACLE MOUNTAIN (FORMERLY MAUMELLE MOUNTAIN)

THE GRAND PRAIRIE

THE RIVER AT LITTLE ROCK

DREDGING ALONG THE ARKANSAS

COMMON GALLINULE COURTSHIP

is sixteen feet. In 1986, the river covered the lock walls. The lockmaster said he had seen that happen three times in fourteen years. And he has seen the flow as high as 400,000 cubic feet per second!

Freight had been carried by flatboat and keel boat until the steamboat *Comet* made it up to Arkansas Post in 1820. Then in the spring of 1822, the *Eagle* arrived at the village of Little Rock. During the 1830s the famous Captain Henry Shreve, who had cleared the Red River, was at work on the Arkansas, removing snags. Steamboats were even carrying wheat and flour from Kansas to Arkansas during high water. By 1872, at least 117 steamboats had been lost on the river. A few had gone down because of boiler explosions, but most went down because of snags.

By 1884, steamboat traffic was on its way out because the railroad had been completed from Little Rock to Ft. Smith. River traffic would not resume until the opening of the McClellan-Kerr Navigation System in 1970.

From Little Rock on downriver, the land flattens and we have entered the world of the delta. For much of the way, we are strangely back in prairie country, the half-million acres known as the Grand Prairie. Today virtually all the native prairie has been plowed under and committed to rice production. At the time of settlement, however, the big bluestem, the Indian grass, and the switchgrass were as tall as a man.

Mike had to leave this river journey in Pine Bluff. He had been engaged to design the sets for a coming production in Pine Bluff and had to make a presentation the next morning. I knew he was sorry to go, but also knew he had found lots of seeds that would become river poems. I wondered when I would see the first one. I had a rendezvous with Tom Foti the next day to explore Big Island down near the end of the river.

I felt a sense of impending release as we left the landing. The last lock, and the last dam, were gone. The Grand Prairie was gone, too. Now we were entering the dense hardwood bottoms and cypress swamps. And the end of the river. Big Island, bounded on the north by the White River, on the east by the Big Muddy, and on the south by the Arkansas, would be the end of my journey. Like the source on Mt. Arkansas, this area was uninhabited except briefly by deer hunters in the late fall.

The White River was very muddy from rains further north, noticeably more muddy than the Arkansas Post Canal that it joined. Large limbs and logs drifted like some record of a tragedy. The White River in the Ozarks of northwest Arkansas differs as much from what is before us as the mountain stream of the Arkansas in Colorado does from the river in the south. The White is dammed many times before it gets here. One of the negative results of this and the damming of the Arkansas is the drastically reduced numbers of the alligator gar.

WINTER CYPRESS

Gars look like ancient fish, and they are. They got their start in the Mesozoic era. They like warm water and have always done well in the South. Even if the water gets low in the summer, they've got a lung-like swim bladder that can supplement the gills in absorbing oxygen. They like the backwaters and bayous where they feed on shad and minnows. What they couldn't adapt to was the sudden releases of cold tailwaters from the dams. That and channelization. So after a couple of hundred million years they may be on their way out. Some alligator gars have grown to nine feet and over three hundred pounds! Lots of fishermen think they're still abundant, but they mistake them for the three other kinds of gars in the Arkansas and the White. If the alligator gars disappear completely, the river will never be the same.

For roughly two and a half miles we were running through the southernmost end of the White River National Wildlife Refuge, some 113,000 acres of ox-bow lakes and swamps. It's forested with lots of gum, willow, and oaks, but also that special tree, the bald cypress. It is unique to this end of the river, just like the alligator gar that cruises slowly by the tree's "knees," roots raised above the water. Also like the gar, the bald cypress is of very ancient lineage. The bald, which is not a member of the cypress family, but instead the redwood family, is like the redwood very resistant to insects and disease. One has only to enter the green, dark world of a cypress swamp and maybe see an alligator's eyes just above the surface, to sense a different species of mystery, one very different from that felt on the high alpine tundra of Colorado. For it is only in such a place that life can diversify so fecundly, a place positioned just right between fire and ice.

Because of the refuge's uneven southern boundary, we entered the refuge a second time briefly between the Missouri-Pacific railroad bridge and the Mississippi. On the way Tom Foti took some photos of the logging that was going on. Several barges had been brought upriver and were heavily loaded with persimmon on its way to be made into golf clubs. These logs were from private land that fell between the uneven boundaries.

I knew we would not see them today, as we roared along in an outboard, but part of what's left of the cougar lives in the refuge, where there is also black bear and a large deer population. Although I have seen jaguar in Nicaragua (and been followed by one at night), I have never seen a cougar in the wilds in my native country. The chances grow fewer every day. In Florida, one is more likely to see one that has been hit by a speeding car at night. Here, at least, there are no highways. Even though I haven't seen a cougar, I am happy to know they are here.

We passed the navigational marker, Birmingham Bend Light, then sped along the last straight stretch before the Big Muddy. Around Big Island Light, Tom looked ahead and

WHITE PELICAN

WHITE PELICANS

FLOODED HARDWOOD BOTTOMS

MALLARDS

GREAT WHITE EGRETS AND YOUNG

ALLIGATORS SUCH AS THIS HAVE BEEN RELEASED AT HOLLA BEND
AND WHITE RIVER NATIONAL WILDLIFE REFUGE

GREAT SANDBARS NEAR THE MOUTH OF THE ARKANSAS

shouted above the engine noise, "Look at the difference in the color of the Mississippi . . . now that's muddy." From a distance he had been fooled, just as I had been the previous year. As we drew to the mouth of the White, the light color turned out to be the sloping side of a great sand bar on the east bank of the Mississippi. We were both exhilarated coming suddenly upon the expanse of a great bend in the Mississippi added to the mouth of the White. As I hit the turbulence where the two rivers met, I suddenly felt the boat start swivel-hipping when the swirling water hit the motor's shaft. It was much more obvious with my hand on the wheel and for seconds I feared it might be enough to flip us.

We turned south for a mile and then Tom motioned us up the channel of the old White. He wanted to check a tract of land that he had observed a year ago, to take a more careful look now. It was being offered by a private owner for sale to the state of Arkansas. High above us in the blue summer sky an eastern kingbird was attacking a red-shouldered hawk. Not only would he dive close to him; he landed on the red-shoulder's back and seemed to stay glued there for ten seconds.

Much of the bank in the bends where Tom thought the tract lay was high, but finally we found where we could land. As we stumbled up the bank, small willows were holding the sandy soil. And then we entered the canopy of the woods. Tom pointed at the undulations of the forest floor and remarked, "This is a classic example of a point bar in the meandering river, gradually building and adding new ground. As it continues to pile up sediment, it creates a kind of ridge that holds itself back, then starts all over again. It's called 'swell and swale.'"

I like the sound of the word "swale." It echoes its likely past in Icelandic and is akin to the Old Norse word meaning "a shady, cool place." Our swale here on Big Island was shady and cooler than the open river. Today the word *swale* is reserved for "low and moist." There is little undergrowth where we walk, because the towering cottonwoods, sycamores, and sugarberry trees shut out much of the light.

The formation of bars starts with the river meandering, changing, and leaving its rich load of sediment. The development of these bars is inextricably tied to plant succession. Sometimes there may be sandbar willows at first. It's a chancy beginning and a portion of the crown must stay out of water long enough to get a start. In several years the young willows stop more and more sediment, more and more sand, and finally a bar gets started. But maybe the sand bar willow is not the beginning; maybe the black willow and cottonwood go straight to work. These species are old friends all along the river, way up through western Kansas and eastern Colorado, because they like moist country. As a matter of fact, even when we leave the soil of Colorado and head into the Rockies where there is less soil, and a higher altitude, a member of the family takes over, the aspen, which also resides in the same genus, *Populus*. Yet another connection holding the community of the Arkansas together.

The cottonwoods deep in the woods were towering. Tom had brought an "increment borer" which he uses to bore into a tree and draw a sample. It was only fourteen inches long and the diameter of one hoary old cottonwood we estimated at about forty inches. Even within the

EASTERN TENT CATERPILLARS

fourteen inches of sample we counted there were fifty-five rings. Extrapolating for the other six inches of the radius, Tom estimated about eighty years for the specimen. Water poured from the hole even as he bored in, and he exclaimed, "Boy, this water stinks." Even the part of the borer that he offered for smelling had a strong odor, but we noticed that deeper within the heart of the tree the smell was not as bad. The wood was denser there.

The great cottonwoods were indications, and partial cause, of what followed in the succession (which is still going on). As the cottonwoods grow taller and fuller, they create the shade we were enjoying, but this same shade keeps other species that are not very shade tolerant from starting their way upward and outward in the world. Willows and cottonwoods have an advantage for awhile by getting off the ground more quickly. After twenty years or so, the willows begin to decline, having lost the race upward to the cottonwoods. While this is going on, box elder and red maple are catching on because they can make it in the shade, which is a good way to make it if you can. Gradually, through the great round of the year, then the years, the soil gets richer from the fallen leaves, the bodies and droppings of animals, which are in turn reworked by bacteria, earthworms, and a host of other small creatures. Although sugarberry, sycamore, elm, and sweet gum are not excessive shade lovers, they manage to get their start because of the soil enriched by years of life and death among small plants and animals. On this particular part of Big Island we saw abundant sweet gum and sugarberry (which I had grown up calling "hackberry," and whose designation is properly *Celtis occidentalis*), and the occasional honey locust. In light of the progress of the succession, plus Tom's sample boring of the big cottonwood, we knew we were in roughly an eighty-year-old virgin forest. "Virgin" forest is an accurate term because this forest began on new ground and not from plowed-over ground that had been permitted to fall back to forest.

The virgin's progress would be as follows: the dominance of the cottonwoods would give way to the sugarberry and sweet gum; then as the virgin ages, pecan or the oaks and hickories get a hold. Water tolerance no doubt has much to do with what stays. In the interior of Big Island, which is older than the point bar that we walked on now, overcup oak has the upper hand, along with water hickory and another hickory, the pecan. Still with the mature virgin forest are the sugarberries and sweet gums. One oak that does not predominate, but is in evidence, is the Nuttall.

As we turned into the old White River Tom had told me that it was really *this* White River that Thomas Nuttall had entered. During January, Nuttall turned away from the Mississippi and entered this channel (or close by) and came to a bayou, which he didn't name, and from this bayou he entered the Arkansas.

Although there were few emigrants anywhere, knavery had made its quick way to the Mississippi and even to the Arkansas. His entry for the 13th of January begins:

Today I was detained at Mr. M'Lane's, waiting the drunken whim of the Yankee, whom necessity had obliged me to hire. In the course of a few hours he had shifted from two bargains. At first, I was to give him five dollars for his assistance, and in case that should prove inadequate, I had agreed to hire an additional hand on the Arkansas. Now he wished to have the boat for bringing her completely to the Port, and next he wanted 10 dollars!

In the very next entry he writes:

I now found the boatman whom I had hired, one of the most worthless and drunken scoundrels imaginable; he could not be prevailed upon to do any thing but steer, while myself and the other man I had hired, were obliged to keep constantly to the oar, or the cordelle.

Yes, a cordelle, or tow-rope, because Nuttall was taking a boat upstream. On this particular day they pulled it "only" six and a half miles. When many of us have these seizures of retroactive pioneering and try doing without the internal combustion engine, we probably see ourselves paddling canoes *down* river. But if you live in a place there is a going and a coming back, and the coming back, if it's up a river, can be tedious and hard. Numerous entries find Nuttall waist or shoulder deep in the muddy Arkansas, pulling his flatboat behind him. And he was paying.

It took Nuttall a week to get from the bayou's mouth to Arkansas Post, where he was to remain for a little more than a month. The original post had been established in 1686 by La Salle's lieutenant, Henry de Tonti. At this time the post was just several miles from the mouth of the Arkansas. Because of flooding it was twice moved, the final place the one where Nuttall visited. At the time there were about thirty or forty houses. The French had held the post until 1764, after which it remained under the Spanish flag until 1800. From 1803 it became American with the Louisiana Purchase. From the time Nuttall left the post to move upstream, a week would pass before it became the territorial capital of Arkansas on March 2, 1819.

We are in former Quapaw country, and it was in these parts that Nuttall talked to some of them. The Quapaw had split off from other Dhegiha Sioux and come down the Mississippi, ultimately to stop at the mouth of the Arkansas. Thus their name, which means "Down Stream People." I have not run across a derogatory description of the Quapaw anywhere. They were quite happy to get along with the French and enjoyed the company of white men in general. For all this, they were poorly used. Nuttall notes of them that "they say, that in consequence of their mildness and love of peace, they have been overlooked by the Americans, [who] are ready enough to conciliate by presents those who are in danger of becoming their enemies, but neglect those who are their unchangeable friends."

The Americans were soon up to their old bargaining tricks and in a treaty shown Nuttall by Chief Ha-kat-ton, the Americans had traded four thousand dollars down and one thousand dollars a year for 60,000 square miles of land. This was just a start, however, to a very sad story. In 1824 the Quapaw were forced to move to the Red River on some mediocre land of the Caddo, which flooded. Gradually, they straggled forlornly back to what had been their old reservation in order, as one of them put it, to die. The remainder of the Quapaw were removed to Ottawa County in northeast Oklahoma. Their tragedy resulted from American intent.

ARKANSAS POST CANAL

Much earlier, as they were first contacted by Europeans in the sixteenth and seventeenth centuries, their people were ravaged by smallpox and other infectious diseases which they had no resistance to. By the time Nuttall saw them they were reduced to only five or six hundred people.

Before the Europeans came the Quapaw were sometimes at odds with their neighbors over boundaries but they appeared to have lived in concert with the natural world, not taking more than was needed. It is true that they did not have the technology to take more than they needed or to ravage the rivers and forest. They grew corn; and understanding that they were not the absolute rulers of the world, they asked that their efforts be blessed before they planted and after they harvested. They gathered fruit and nuts from the forest, and probably fed themselves mainly from hunting and fishing. In an ambivalent compliment, Nuttall observes that "as to the future state, in which they are firm believers, their ideas are merely deduced from what they see around them. Their heaven for hunters is at least as rational as that of some of our own fanatics."

Deeper in the woods, still walking over swell and swale, I wondered if I was near the old bank of the river where Nuttall had perhaps walked. The place where Tom had made his boring had surely been river bed then. A hundred and sixty-eight years ago maybe we would have needed to be deeper in the woods, where the oaks were. At any rate, it's pleasant to have the benevolent ghost of Nuttall walking along, as he has been since Oklahoma.

Soon we returned to our boat and decided to take the chance on a run out the Old White to the Mississippi and then back up the Arkansas. Chancy for several reasons, foremost of which was the danger of running out of gas. From the looks of the traffic, which was nearly zero, we would be left to our own devices if we became stranded. We might get a feel for Nuttall's trip the hard way.

In a very short time we could see the Mississippi through an opening between a couple of treed sandbars, but we passed that outlet, speeding for the real mouth. We saw the great sweep of the Mississippi before us, the wind keeping us cool at the fast clip of the old Johnson. And then we went aground. Really aground. For the longest time I tried to raise the motor so that we could drift in the current until we reached the channel of the Mississippi. After many appropriate words of benediction, there was nothing left to do but go over the side.

Somehow I had not only buried the prop in the soft sand, I had also fouled the release mechanism that raises the motor. After some underwater mechanic work I could raise the motor, but the current was unexpectedly strong and I nearly lost Tom and the boat. We needed to go back upstream to the earlier outlet, so there was nothing for Tom Foti to do but heave himself over the side, too, as we felt the powerful surge of the Old White trying to join the Father of Waters. The wake of a passing towboat completed the baptism, as we both hung onto the boat and ourselves.

Back in the boat and now in the Mississippi, our wet bodies cooled as we swept along bends a half-mile to a mile long. After ten miles we came to the biggest sand bar I think I've ever

GREAT WHITE EGRET

THE ARKANSAS MEETS OLD MAN RIVER

DEER NEAR MOUTH OF THE ARKANSAS

seen, and it had been built by the Arkansas. Having run aground once already we skipped the shallow opening upstream of the bar. A couple of least terns skimmed by, their heads cocked for the best chance below them.

Finally we were back in our own river. I knew then that this part of the undammed, unlocked, unmanaged river was a different world than the one I had just flown over for hundreds of miles. It's the size of the sand bars that first takes your breath away. The Arkansas Natural Scenic River Commission realized what a treasure it had and now it's officially scenic. Here was proof enough that nature likes a curve better than a straight line.

We saw two wild turkeys looking like a couple of gaited horses as they hoofed it along the sand and disappeared. Passing more such miracles, we soon realized we had to beach the boat. Get out and walk around. Still damp from our recent baptism, we walked across the sun-dazzling sand being cooled by the breeze. Up over a small, natural levee topped with willows, we entered what seemed like a green cathedral of arching willows and cottonwoods. While Tom was checking out his trees, I followed the tracks of armadillo, rabbit, and raccoon. I felt again the great power of diversity in the lower river, life climbing through levels of itself. The deeper we entered the woods, the more variety we found.

Returning to the bar, Tom walked ahead until he froze, his hand reaching out in warning. He whispered that a deer was in a huge pile of river debris ahead. "I'll go around the other side," he said, and moved glacially slow around the uprooted trees and disappeared from my sight. Only the warblers behind us made any sound. Then she exploded across the sand, making for the woods. In one great tawny, arcing leap, she demanded not to die out, just to be let be.

WORKS CITED

Campbell, Joseph. *The Masks of God: Primitive Mythology*. New York, 1982.

Collins, Joseph T., ed. *Natural Kansas*. Lawrence, KS, 1985.

Foti, Thomas L. *The Natural Divisions of Arkansas*. Little Rock, 1979.

Fremont, John Charles. *Narratives of Exploration and Adventure*. Edited by Allan Nevins. New York, 1956.

Griffin, James B. "An Interpretation of the Place of Spiro in Southeastern Archaeology," in *The Missouri Archaeologist*. Columbia, 1952.

Hardin, Garrett. "The Tragedy of the Commons," in *Science*. Washington, D.C., 1968.

Hilgartner, Stephen, ed. *Nukespeak: The Selling of Nuclear Technology in America*. San Francisco, 1982.

Jackson, Donald, ed. *The Journals of Zebulon Montgomery Pike*. Norman, OK, 1966.

Mathews, John Joseph. *The Osage*. Norman, OK, 1982.

Matthiessen, Peter. *Wildlife in America*. New York, 1978.

Mayhall, Mildred P. *The Kiowas*. Norman, OK, 1984.

Mills, William. *Bears and Men: A Gathering*. Chapel Hill, 1986.

Nuttall, Thomas. *A Journal of Travels into the Arkansas Territory During the Year 1819*. Edited by Savoie Lottinville. Norman, OK, 1979.

Orr, David. "What the Future Holds: The Prospects of Appropriate Technology," in *Meadowcreek Notes*, #12. Fox, AR, 1986.

Ranney, Dave. *Garden City (Kansas) Telegram*, August 11, 1987.

Rubin, Louis D. *The Even-Tempered Angler*. New York, 1983.

Simmons, Marc. *Following the Santa Fe Trail*. Santa Fe, 1986.

Voynick, Stephen. "Yesterday's Mines," in *American Forests*. Washington, D.C., Feb., 1984.

Webb, Walter Prescott. *The Great Plains*. Lincoln, NE, 1981.

INDEX